STAGE DIRECTORS HANDBOOK

OPPORTUNITIES FOR DIRECTORS AND CHOREOGRAPHERS

Prepared by
Stage Directors and
Choreographers Foundation

David Diamond and Terry Berliner
Editors

Theatre Communications Group • New York

This publication is made possible in part with public funds from the New York State Council
on the Arts, a State Agency.

Stage directors handbook : opportunities for directors and choreographers/
prepared by Stage Directors and Choreographers Foundation;
David Diamond and Terry Berliner, editors.
p. cm.
Includes index.
ISBN 1-55936-150-6 (alk. paper)
1. Theater—Production and direction—Vocational guidance.
I. Diamond, David. II. Berliner, Terry.
III. Stage Directors and Choreographers Foundation.
PN2053.S68   1998
792'.0233'023—dc21   98-16284
CIP

Book design and typography by Peter Lukic

First Edition, December 1998

STAGE
DIRECTORS
HANDBOOK

Contents

Acknowledgments

Special thanks to the theatrical community, and many specific members of that community, who have contributed their expertise to this Handbook: Michèle Assaf (Director/Choreographer), Douglas Carter Beane (Artistic Director, the Drama Dept.), Claudia Catania (Executive Producer, The New Group), Martha Coigney (Executive Director, International Theatre Institute), Jeremy Dobrish (Artistic Director, adobe Theatre Company), Anne Fliotsos (University of Missouri Columbia, Missouri), Peter Hagan (Agent, Gersh Agency), Julie Hamberg (Director), W. E. Scott Hoot, Esq., Moisés Kaufman (Playwright/Artistic Director, Tectonic Theater Project), Roberta Levitow (Director), Christopher Martin (Director/Designer), Greg McCaslin (Program Director, Center for Arts Education), Robert Moss (Artistic Director, Syracuse Stage), Sharon Ott (Artistic Director, Seattle Repertory Theatre), Marshall B. Purdy (Associate Producer, Walt Disney Theatricals), Sacha Reich (Director), Jeffrey Richards (Press Agent, Jeffrey Richards Associates), Stephen A. Schrum (University of Charlston, West Virginia).

For volunteering time, collecting and checking listings, and helping in many, many valuable ways, we greatly appreciate the contributions of Beau Bernarda, Kathryn Haapala, Bob Johnson, Jacqueline Kleefield and Jim O'Quinn. We thank the incredibly supportive staff at TCG Books: Peter Lukic, Terry Nemeth, Steven Samuels and Kathy Sova, for helping us put this resource guide together in the most logical and useful way.

David Diamond and Terry Berliner
November 1998

FOREWORD

Welcome to the first *Stage Directors Handbook*! At last there's one resourse to go to for the information you need. It has taken many years of painstaking work to get us here. It is, for me, a dream fulfilled.

For the past six years or so, I have been asked the same questions over and over again. Where can I get information about grant opportunities, assistant jobs, agents, international festivals, producing my own plays? It has been my dream to provide one place where all that information could be accessed easily and quickly. That's where the idea for this volume began.

It started out as an appendix to the recently redesigned *Journal for Stage Directors and Choreographers*, which, six years ago, did not include much practical information for the working professional. We added a resource guide to one issue and then the next and the next. (If you are not familiar with the *Journal*, you should be: there you will read discussions on craft, case histories of important productions, inspirational talks with leaders of the industry, reports on major phenomena that affect the theatre, and updates to the resources you find in this book.) Then I thought it would be great to assemble all the resource guides into a single book, giving you one place to look for the organization, helpful hint, theatre, etc., that you need to reference. One easy-to-use guide.

And, in addition to the cold, hard facts, we've also included experiences and advice from practitioners in the field. It's fine to have a list of agents who represent directors, but when is the right time in your career to approach one to represent you and how do you manage it? Throughout the year, the SDC Foundation sponsors meetings to answer such questions. Here we have included excerpts from some of those discussions.

I'm sure there is much more information that you will need as you navigate your career as a director or choreographer in the theatre. Here is a starting point. We hope to revise and update this book biennially so that the information will be as up-to-date as possible. We rely on your input to enrich and improve future editions.

There are many opportunities out there for theatre directors and choreographers, but there always seems to be more of you than can be accommodated. So, we looked for alternatives to traditional stage productions. Some of you will be attracted to new media, so we have included a chapter on directing for the Internet. (Of course, by the time you read this, there will be new technologies to explore.) I should note that it is not our intention to turn anyone away from the theatre. But we know that most of you are not working all the time, and when you aren't, it may be preferable to "direct" a CD-ROM or an interactive game, than to pursue less creative alternative work.

This handbook furthers the ongoing goals of the SDC Foundation. We approach the millenium with a broad mission: to be communication central for directors and choreographers, to provide information and resources that will help you grow as an artist, while helping you grow more savvy in the ways of this business. It's not always easy to do both; we hope we've saved you at least one step along the way.

David Diamond
Executive Director
SDC Foundation

Introduction
Navigating Your Career
By Moisés Kaufman

When David Diamond and Terry Berliner of SDC Foundation called and asked me to write the introduction to this book, they told me that it should focus on "how one navigates one's career." I must admit I was rather surprised and slightly amused. I have never been very good at working on "my career" (and "navigating" sounds like the type of athletic activity to which I'm allergic). Whenever I have tried working on my career, I have only succeeded in making all the wrong decisions. Instead, the focus for me has always been to try and do the work I feel passionate about, which in my case has always revolved around theatrical language and form, and to work with people who share this interest.

So I felt rather awkward about writing this introduction. However, I started to look at the path I have taken in my work, and the truth is: I can see a pattern, a set of decisions that have led me to where I am today. I guess one would call this a "career." I also remembered the panic I felt when I arrived in the United States with the desire to create theatre, and the sense of being completely lost about how to do that.

So when David sent me the material he was using in this volume, I thought, "Yes, this will be a very useful book." It will provide a map, a guide, to the many resources available to directors. Once you have decided on the kind of work that interests you as a director, and the kind of questions you are interested in asking in that work, this book will prove a great tool in guiding you to the opportunities to do just that.

By the time I got to New York in 1987, I had been working for five years as an actor in a theatre company in my native Venezuela. It was a company that was greatly influenced by contemporary directors like Peter Brook, Jerzy Grotowski and Pina Bausch—great theatrical innovators that really influenced the way we created work and conducted our rehearsals.

It was there I decided I wasn't very interested in being an actor, in creating one character. I was much more interested in creating the whole stage event. At the same time, I was also coming to terms with my sexuality, and Venezuela was not a place where one could be gay and lead a healthy life. So I decided to move to New York. (It's interesting how many of the "career decisions" we make in our lives sometimes have very little to do with professional choices.)

Once here, I started looking for a place to study, or rather, to develop techniques which would allow me to create on the stage the work I was creating in my head. After trying several schools and studios, a friend recommended the Experimental Theater Wing at New York University. He said it would be a good place for me to study. So I talked to Wendell Beavers, who was leading the program then, and told him I wanted space and actors to develop new works, while taking classes. He said I could do that kind of work at ETW, and so I enrolled. There, I directed several plays as well as created new works. It was then that I started to formulate both the questions and the methodology that we are still using today in my company, Tectonic Theater Project (TTP).

After two years, I went to Arthur Bartow, then Head of the Drama Department at NYU, and asked him: "How does one get work in this field?" He was very gentle: "You are going to have a hard time because of the kind of work you do. Because of the kind of research you are doing in the theatre, the kind of exploration you are doing, you are probably going to have to create your own company."

While a student at the ETW, I had followed the work of several downtown theatre companies in New York. So his idea made sense. I realized that the work I was interested in would need that kind of an environment in order to mature and grow.

But, first I wanted to see other directors at work. (Who was it that said that directing is like sex, one never sees other people doing it?) I had questions not so much about the craft of directing but about the craft of creating a room, creating an atmosphere where questions can be asked. I decided to assist people whose work I admired. I worked with Steve Wangh, as he created a new music theatre piece with students at NYU, and I also went to Israel to work with Rina Yerushalmi on her acclaimed production of *Hamlet*. This period was terrific for me. As an assistant, I observed how these two very seasoned directors went about creating work and making a space where that work was possible.

After a year of assistant directing, I felt I was ready. I decided to create a laboratory where I could explore the theatrical ideas that interested me. Tectonic Theater Project, a company dedicated to producing work that explores theatrical language and form, was born.

At that time, my lover was running an AIDS education program. This meant he had a regular salary, which meant he could request a bank loan. We requested. We got a loan for $10,000, and proceeded to produce our first play: *Women in Beckett*—the entire collection of Samuel Beckett's short plays for women. It was well received and started us off on a good note. A year later we applied for and received not-for-profit status.

Starting Tectonic was the best decision of my life. It helped ground me. Many of the questions about how to do the work were answered (of course a hundred other questions came up). But the centering effect that the company had on me was terrific. This was a place were I could do my work, where I could collaborate with other artists over a long period of time. Now I must warn you—this is not for everyone. We did all of the producing work in the company—everything from fundraising to marketing to press representation. They were exciting times but we were working twelve to fourteen hour days.

I went to Jim Nicola (Artistic Director of New York Theater Workshop) and asked him how I could get a strong financial base for the company. He said: "Governmental sources have dried up. So you better get private sources of funding. Get people who want to support the kind of work you're doing." This advice was invaluable. At a time when other theatre companies floundered, TTP survived because we weren't dependant on government grants.

TTP has been alive now for six years. From the beginning, we have done the kind of work we always wanted to do. Now we receive public funding. But, even so, our latest production, *Gross Indecency: The Three Trials of Oscar Wilde*, was a difficult one. It had a cast of nine and took two years to create. At first, we felt it was too big a project for Tectonic to produce, so we tried to get a commercial producer interested. We got many refusals. In the end we decided to produce it ourselves. The play has been a great success for us.

As I reread this, it all makes perfect sense. It seems logical—a clean progression. But, the truth is that it wasn't obvious or clear. Those were difficult times—full of doubts, fear and uncertainties. The only thing never uncertain for me was the kind of work I wanted to do, and the kind of questions I wanted to ask. That always remained at the center—the driving force behind the work.

There are many ways to work as a director. Some of my friends have been doing the regional theatre circuit, others have stayed in one theatre and worked their way up, others have started their own companies. The most important thing is: What are the ideas, what are the questions you are posing? This will lead you to design the kind of path you take in constructing your "career." This way, the career will always be the result of the quest, and not the other way around.

Moisés Kaufman
Playwright/Artistic Director
Tectonic Theater Project
New York City, November 1998

STAGE
DIRECTORS
HANDBOOK

CHAPTER 1

DIRECTOR TRAINING PROGRAMS

T here are many approaches that one can take to train and develop skills most useful to directing. This chapter presents programs available throughout the United States which are geared toward developing the aspiring director's technical craft and creative vision. Programs range from one- to two-day workshops to three-year Master of Fine Arts degrees. This list does not represent all workshops and degree programs, but will serve as a starting point to the possibilities that exist. This chapter is divided into sections: Graduate College, University and Certificate Programs; Undergraduate College and University Programs; and Directing Workshops. Listings are in alphabetical order by name of school or workshop. Each listing contains address information, the length of the program, application deadline, approximate cost (for workshops only) and a brief description of program. Most university programs have Web Sites that are extremely helpful for quick information on curriculum, faculty and more. Application deadlines listed here are subject to change. Always contact program directly for guidelines and deadlines.

GRADUATE COLLEGE, UNIVERSITY AND CERTIFICATE

The following two- and three-year director-training programs culminate in either a certificate, a Master of Fine Arts (M.F.A.) degree or a Ph.D. degree.

American Repertory Theatre
Institute for Advanced Theatre Training at Harvard University/
Moscow Art Theatre (MXAT) School
A.R.T. Institute for Advanced Theatre Training
64 Brattle St; Cambridge, MA 02138
(617) 495-2668; 495-1705 FAX
Web: http://www.fas.harvard.edu/~art/
François Rochaix, Director of A.R.T. IATT

Degree: Certificate of Achievement from Harvard University or M.F.A. from MXAT. **Length of program:** 2 years (5 semesters). **Application deadline:** Jan 19. **Program:** An intensive program where each student directs workshops and fully rendered productions, in addition to participating in the work of the A.R.T. A term will be spent at the MXAT School, where directors will train under established Russian directors, assist a director through production and continue the study of theatre history and literature.

Boston University
School for the Arts—Theatre Arts Department
855 Commonwealth Ave, Room 470; Boston, MA 02215
(617) 353-3350; 353-4363 FAX
Web: http://web.bu.edu/SFA/theatre/theatrehome.html
Eve B. Muson, Executive Assistant Director of Performance

Degree: M.F.A. **Length of program:** 3 years. **Application deadline:** Jan 15. **Program:** Encourages directors to extend, intensify and focus their theatrical sensibilities. The general orientation of the program stems from Theatre Arts' conviction that one learns how to direct by directing. The resident professional company at B.U. is the Huntington Theatre Company.

Brooklyn College of the City University of New York
Theater Department
317 Whitehead Hall; 2900 Bedford Ave; Brooklyn, NY 11210
(718) 951-5666; 951-4606 FAX
E-mail: sleiter@brooklyn.cuny.edu
Web: http://depthome.brooklyn.cuny.edu/theater
Tom Bullard, Head of Directing

Degree: M.F.A. **Length of program:** 2 years. **Application deadline:** May.
Program: Trains directors to perform with distinction and leadership in the professional theatre. Students are given a variety of opportunities beyond the strict requirements of the program to explore their vision and extend their connections to the professional world. They are encouraged to produce and direct performances for the Lunch Time Theatre, as well as off-campus venues. Qualified students are often placed as paid interns at leading theatre institutions in New York City.

California Institute of the Arts
24700 McBean Parkway; Valencia, CA 91355
(805) 253-7863; 254-8352 FAX
Kenneth Young, Director of Admissions
Travis Preston, Head of Directing for Theatre
Lou Florimonte, Head of Directing for Theatre Video and Cinema

Degree: M.F.A. **Length of program:** 3 years. **Application deadline:** Mid-Jan. **Program:** Offers two separate directing programs: one focusing specifically on directing for the theatre, another focusing on video and cinema. Each program strives to develop a strong foundation of skills as well as cultivate an active creative vision for theatre, or video and cinema.

California State University, Fullerton
School of the Arts—Department of Theatre and Dance
Box 6850; Fullerton, CA 92834-6850
(714) 278-3628; 278-7041 FAX
Web: http://www.theatre.Fullerton.edu/
Susan Hallman, Department Chair

Degree: M.F.A. **Length of program:** 3 years. **Application deadline:** Varies.
Program: The goal of the department is the humanistic education and aesthetic training of students in both theory and craft. Includes challenging classroom and production experience, community service and outreach activities, internships with prominent theatres, and film and television studios in Southern California.

Carnegie Mellon University
The School of Drama
5000 Forbes Ave; Pittsburgh, PA 15213-3890
(412) 268-2082; 268-0281 FAX
Web: http://www.cmu.edu/cfa/drama/direct.html
Gregory Lehane, Head of Directing

Degree: M.F.A. **Length of program:** 2 to 3 years, based on experience.
Application deadline: Jan 1. **Program:** Provides in-depth and varied encounters with directing theory and practice, dramatic theory, criticism and history. The student develops the skills needed for successful collaborations with designers, playwrights and actors.

Columbia University
Division of Theatre
MC 1807; 2960 Broadway, Room 601; New York, NY 10027
(212) 854-3408
Anne Bogart, Advisor, M.F.A. Directing Program

Degree: M.F.A. **Length of program:** 3 years. **Application deadline:** Jan 4.
Program: Based on the idea that one's vision as a director is developed through practice, encouragement, critical feedback, collaboration and more practice. The training is project-oriented and offers the director the possibility of working daily with actors, playwrights, dramaturgs, managers and designers.

DePaul University
The Theatre School
2135 North Kenmore; Chicago, IL 60614-4111
(773) 325-7917; 325-7920 FAX
Web: http://theatreschool.depaul.edu/
Jim Ostholthoff, Directing Program Head
Melissa Meltzer, Theatre School Director of Admissions

Degree: M.F.A. **Length of program:** 3 years. **Application deadline:** Jan 15.
Program: Founded as the Goodman School of Drama in 1925, the major thrust of the program emerges from the acting tradition of the Goodman School. The program is committed to "learning by doing" with an emphasis on the relationship of the director to the actor and the text. Students take a variety of classes including acting, art, history, theatrical collaboration (a team-taught class that brings directing and design students together) and dramaturgy along with directing classes. Each student directs approximately 7 productions culminating in a fully supported thesis production in the last year.

Florida Atlantic University
Department of Theatre
777 Glades Rd; Box 3091; Boca Raton, FL 33431-0991
(561) 367-3810; 297-2180 FAX
Jean-Louis Baldet, Chair of Acting, Directing, Drama Theory

Degree: M.F.A. **Length of program:** 2 years and an internship. **Application deadline:** Jun 1. **Program:** Offers students practical opportunities along with comprehensive classroom training. Students direct one-act and full-length plays, are encouraged to assist faculty and guest artist directors on stage productions, and are required to stage manage at least one mainstage production. The final directing project is a full-length play which serves as the student's directorial thesis.

Florida State University
School of Theatre
327 Fine Arts Building; Tallahassee, FL 32306-1160
(850) 644-6795; 644-7408 FAX
Web: http://www.fsu.edu/~theatre/
Frank Trezza, Academic Coordinator

Degree: M.F.A. **Length of program:** 3 years. **Application deadline:** Does not accept directing students every year. Call for information. **Program:** Combines classroom experience with production assignments and internships. The direction of a juried thesis production is required for graduation.

Humboldt State University
Theatre Arts Department
1 Harpst St; Arcata, CA 95521
(707) 826-3566; 826-5494 FAX
Web: http://www.humboldt.edu/~theatre/
Bernadette Cheyne, Department Chair

Degree: M.F.A. **Length of program:** 3 years. **Application deadline:** For fall enrollment: Mar 15; for spring enrollment: Oct 15. **Program:** Provides rigorous professional training in theatrical and/or film directing; encourages boldness and skepticism in theatrical presentation; prepares the student to recognize the difference between imitation, interpretation and creative style; and prepares the student to accept responsibility and leadership in American theatre.

Illinois State University
Department of Theatre
Campus Box 5700; Normal, IL 61790-5700
(309) 438-8783; 438-7214 FAX
E-mail: theatre@oratmail.cfa.ilstu.edu
Web: http://orathost.cfa.ilstu.edu/theatre/
Calvin MacLean, Head of Directing Area

Degree: M.F.A. **Length of program:** 3 years. **Application deadline:** Mar.
Program: Emphasizes strong theoretical foundation and commitment to the
value of artistic research. The student in directing will also benefit from Illinois State's direct ties to the professional theatre in Chicago, and its association with the Illinois Shakespeare Festival.

Indiana University
Department of Theatre and Drama
Theatre 200; Bloomington, IN 47405
(812) 855-4503; 855-4704 FAX
E-mail: thtr@kubrick.fa.indiana.edu
Web: http://www.fa.indiana.edu/~thtr/
Howard Jensen, Head of Acting and Directing Program

Degree: M.F.A. **Length of program:** 3 years. **Application deadline:** Feb. **Program:** Structured for students who intend to pursue professional careers in theatre as either scholars or artists. The department operates three theatres, providing ample opportunity for practical application of skills learned in classes.

Juilliard School
Drama Division
Andrew W. Mellon Foundation Directors Program
60 Lincoln Center Plaza; New York, NY 10023-6588
(212) 799-5000
Web: http://www.juilliard.edu/
JoAnne Akalaitis, Michael Kahn and Garland Wright, Co-Directors

Degree: Graduate level fellowships. **Length of program:** 3 years. **Application deadline:** Dec. **Program:** Three tuition-free fellowships available. In addition to assisting professional directors, Fellows participate in weekly seminars with the program's co-directors, participate in collaborative performance projects and attend related classes at New York University. Directing Fellows will direct student productions and participate in an assistantship with a professional New York production.

Louisiana State University
Department of Theatre
217 Music and Dramatic Arts Building; Baton Rouge, LA 70803
(504) 388-4174; 388-4135 FAX
Web: http://www.artsci.lsu.edu/theatre/graduate.html
Barry Kyle, Head of Graduate Directing Program

Degree: M.F.A. **Length of program:** 3 years. **Application deadline:** Ongoing. **Program:** Specializes in the highly individualized instruction of professional stage directors. Strong emphasis is placed on developing creative thought, self-motivation and intellectual inquiry.

Mankato State University
Theatre Arts Department
Box 8400; Mankato, MN 56002-8400
(507) 389-2118; 389-2922 FAX
Web: http://www.internet-connections.net/web2/msuth/
Dr. Paul Hustoles, Department Chair

Degree: M.F.A. **Length of program:** 2 years. **Application deadline:** Mar. **Program:** Offers 5 mainstage productions during the academic year, along with a 3-play summer season and 2 laboratory theatres. Each student is required to complete an internship with a theatrical company approved by the department.

Northwestern University
School of Speech—Department of Theatre
Theatre and Interpretation Center, Room 200; Evanston, IL 60208-2430
(847) 491-3170; 467-2019 FAX
Web: http://www.nwu.edu/speech/departments/theatre.html.
Erwin Beyer, Chair

Degree: M.F.A. **Length of program:** 3 years. **Application deadline:** Mid-Mar. **Program:** Includes a structured curriculum based on text analysis, collaboration and a variety of directing skills, augmented by numerous production opportunities to educate directors for professional careers. Students are exposed to a wide range of artists, scholars and critical points of view, and engage in close tutorial relationships with a core faculty of recognized active professionals, who are committed to teaching.

Ohio University
School of Theatre—Professional Director Training Program
Kantner Hall 307; Athens, OH 45701-2979
(740) 593-4818; 593-4817 FAX
Web: http://www.cats.ohiou.edu/~thardept/programs/mfadir.htm
Jorge Cacheiro, Head, Professional Director Training Program

Degree: M.F.A. **Length of program:** 3 years. **Application deadline:** Mid-Apr. **Program:** Training is centered around the principle of collaboration with actors, designers and playwrights. Individual student's talent, background and professional goals determine specific elements of the program outside the core requirements. In the third year, along with directing a fully supported main stage project, both domestic and European internships are provided.

Pennsylvania State University
School of Theatre Arts
103 Arts II Building; University Park, PA 16802
(814) 865-7586; 865-7140 FAX
Web: http://www.personal.psu.edu/dept/theatrearts/degrees/direct/direct.html
Dan Carter, Director of the School of Theatre Arts

Degree: M.F.A. **Length of program:** 3 years. **Application deadline:** Mid-Feb. **Program:** Emphasis is placed on nurturing and training each artist as an individual. Provides constant practical directing experience. Each graduate director is expected to be in preparation for, or engaged in rehearsal for, a scene, a new play, a studio project or a mainstage production, every day during his or her 3 years of training.

Roosevelt University
Theatre Department
430 South Michigan Ave; Chicago, IL 60605
(312) 341-3719; 341-3814 FAX
Joel G. Fink, Director of Theatre

Degree: M.F.A. **Length of program:** 3 years. **Application deadline:** Varies. **Program:** Maintains a partnerships with many of Chicago's theatres, which contribute faculty, guest artists, guest speakers and opportunities for student internships. Wisdom Bridge, Steppenwolf and the Goodman have all participated in creating a professional link between theory and practice in theatre.

Rutgers: The State University of New Jersey
Theatre Arts Department
2 Chapel Dr; New Brunswick, NJ 08901-8527
(732) 932-9891; 932-1409 FAX
Harold Scott, Head of the Directing Program

Degree: M.F.A. **Length of program:** 3 years. **Application deadline:** Apr 15.
Program: Consists of classroom theory and directing, as well as directing for the general public once each semester. Assignments mount in complexity and include an original play by an M.F.A. playwright during the second year. In addition to the full directing curriculum, the candidate will take classes in acting, movement, stage combat, design, theatre history and dramatic literature.

Southern Illinois University at Carbondale
Theatre Department
Carbondale, IL 62901-6608
(618) 453-5741; 453-7582 FAX
Sarah Blackstone, Chair

Degree: M.F.A. **Length of program:** 3 years. **Application deadline:** Varies.
Program: Blends scholarship and practice into an academically based theatre experience, which prepares the student for a career in professional, educational or community theatre. May offer an accelerated M.F.A. program for individuals with professional work experience and a B.A. in theatre.

Syracuse University
Department of Drama
200 Crouse College; Syracuse, NY 13244-1140
(315) 443-3089; 443-1935 FAX
John Adams, Assistant Dean

Degree: M.F.A. **Length of program:** 3 years. **Application deadline:** Mar 1.
Program: Focuses on the application of scholarship to the practice of theatre, rather than the pursuit of scholarship for its own sake. The directing student's program of study is tailored to his professional goals. This department shares a special relationship with the Syracuse Stage, allowing students the opportunity to work at a professional theatre.

Texas Tech University
Department of Theatre and Dance
Box 42061; Lubbock, TX 79409-2061
(806) 742-3601; 742-1338 FAX
Jonathan Marks, Head of Directing Program

Degree: M.F.A. in Acting/Directing; Ph.D. of Fine Arts, concentration in Directing. **Length of program:** 54 credits M.F.A., 63 credits Ph.D. **Application deadline:** Mar 1. **Program:** Emphasis on the creative production process which best serves those students who wish to pursue careers in the professional theatre or teach at the university level. The university operates 2 theatres, each producing 4 to 6 plays a year.

University of Alabama
Department of Theatre and Dance
Box 870239; Tuscaloosa, AL 35487-0239
(205) 348-5283; 348-9048 FAX
Edmond Williams, Department Chair and Head of Directing

Degree: M.F.A. **Length of program:** 3 years. **Application deadline:** Dec. **Program:** Prepares students for work in professional theatre, and for employment in educational theatre programs. Four mainstage and 8 studio productions are offered on campus. In association with Alabama Shakespeare Festival, a 10-play winter stock season, as well as a 7-play summer repertory season, are offered.

University of Arizona
Department of Theatre Arts
Box 210003; Tucson, AZ 85721-0003
(520) 621-7008; 621-2412 FAX
E-mail: theatre@cfa.arizona.edu
Web: http://www.arts.arizona.edu/theatre
Harold Dixon, Head of Acting/Directing

Degree: M.F.A. **Length of program:** 3 years. **Application deadline:** Mar 1. **Program:** Emphasizes a balance between studio training, classroom study, a rigorous Arizona Repertory Theatre season, internships with the Arizona Theatre Company and professional film companies on location in Tucson.

University of California, Irvine
School of the Arts—Drama Department
249 Drama; Irvine, CA 92697-2775
(949) 824-6905
Web: http://www.arts.uci.edu/drama/programs/directing.html
Keith Fowler, Head of Directing Program

Degree: M.F.A. **Length of program:** 3 years. **Application deadline:** Jan 15.
Program: The program emphasizes hands-on directing. Directors stage at least 7 full productions—including fully budgeted second-year and third-year shows. Students meet with mentor directors in private tutorials, and present scene work in the weekly Directors' Lab. Many M.F.A. directors find internships with Equity companies during their tenure at UCI.

University of California, Los Angeles
Department of Theater
Box 951622, Los Angeles, CA 90095-1622
(310) 825-7008; 206-1686 FAX
Web: http://www.theater.ucla.edu/mfadirecting.html
Robert Israel and Richard Rose, Co-Chairs, Graduate Directing Program

Degree: M.F.A. **Length of program:** 3 years. **Application deadline:** Sept 1–Dec 15. **Program:** Directors participate in weekly program seminars to critique projects and consider challenges facing the contemporary theatre. Internships are offered in the third year. Directors master the challenge of new and existing material, short and long forms, and a variety of stage configurations. Additionally, students are introduced to the language of direction for the camera.

University of California, San Diego
Department of Theatre and Dance
9500 Gilman Dr; La Jolla, CA 92093
(619) 534-1046; 534-1080 FAX
E-mail: grad-theatre@ucsd.edu
Web: http://www-theatre.ucsd.edu
Jason Stewart, Interim Graduate Coordinator

Degree: M.F.A. **Length of program:** 3 years. **Application deadline:** Fall.
Program: Strives to achieve the most imaginative synthesis of theory and practice, studio exercise and public performance. La Jolla Playhouse is in residence at UCSD for extended seasons each year.

University of Cincinnati
College—Conservatory of Music
Opera, Musical Theater, Drama and Arts Administration Division
Box 210003; Cincinnati, OH 45221-0003
(513) 556-5462; 556-1028 FAX
Web: http://www.uc.edu/www/ccm/CCMOMDA.html
R. Terrell Finney, Chair, OMDA Division

Degree: M.F.A. **Length of program:** 2 years. **Application deadline:** Varies.
Program: Combines instruction in opera, musical theatre, drama, theatre design
and production, and arts administration within a single division. Students have
the opportunity to share in a wide-ranging scope of classes, major productions,
workshop productions, master classes and internships.

University of Hawaii at Manoa
Department of Theatre and Dance
1770 East-West Rd; Honolulu, HI 96822
(808) 956-7677; 956-4234 FAX
E-mail: theatre@hawaii.edu
Web: http://www2.hawaii.edu/~theatre/00.html
Dr. W. Dennis Carroll, Chair and Director of Graduate Studies

Degree: M.F.A. **Length of program:** 3 years. **Application deadline:** Feb 4
for U.S. citizens; Jan 1 for non U.S. citizens. **Program:** Focuses on the intellectual and social basis of performance, and urges students to develop an awareness of the richness of Asian and Western theatrical cultures at the same time
they learn dedication to the disciplines of the art. UHM is the premiere university in the U.S. for the study of Asian theatre, including performance training in Kabuki, Chinese opera and Indonesian shadow puppet theatre.

University of Iowa
Department of Theatre Arts
138 Theatre Building; Iowa City, IA 52242-1705
(319) 335-2700; 335-3568 FAX
Web: http://www.uiowa.edu/~theatre/
Eric Forsythe, Head of Directing Program

Degree: M.F.A. **Length of program:** 3 years. **Application deadline:** Jan.
Program: Focuses on the development of new plays and the collaborative
effort that is central to that process. The program is highly personal and
respects the previous experience and training of its students, and tailors its
curriculum to serve their needs. Students direct at least 6 full productions.

University of Massachusetts
Department of Theater
Box 32620; 112 Fine Arts Center; Amherst, MA 01003-2620
(413) 545-3490; 577-0025 FAX
Web: http://www.umass.edu/
Julian Olf, Graduate Program Director

Degree: M.F.A. **Length of program:** 3 years. **Application deadline:** Mar 1.
Program: Prepares students to work in resident professional theatres, colleges and universities. Students participate in the Department of Theatre production season, working collaboratively under the guidance of faculty artists, in an average of 5 or 6 fully mounted productions.

University of Memphis
Department of Theatre and Dance
Campus Box 526524; Memphis, TN 38152-6524
(901) 678-2523; 678-4331 FAX
Web: http://www.memphis.edu/
Gloria Baxter, Coordinator of Graduate Studies

Degree: M.F.A. **Length of program:** 3 years. **Application deadline:**
Jan–Feb. **Program:** Emphasis on active study of the directing process from conception of an idea to its implementation. Offers an integrative approach characterized by a relational study of the creative process, the exercise of creative imagination and a practical understanding of the craft. Fosters the development of well-rounded, professional, creative theatre artists.

University of Minnesota
Department of Theatre Arts & Dance
204 Middlebrook Hall; 412 22nd Ave, South; Minneapolis, MN 55455-0424
(612) 625-6699
Web: http://cla.umn.edu/theater/mfadirect.html
C. Lance Brockman, Chair

Degree: M.F.A. **Length of program:** 3 years. **Application deadline:** Jan 15.
Program: Emphasis is on hands-on experience. Students direct during the university theatre's mainstage season, and are voting members of the theatre space entirely operated by students. The third year includes a fully staged thesis project and an internship with one of the larger professional theatres in the Twin Cities, including The Guthrie Theater and Penumbra Theatre Company.

University of Mississippi
College of Liberal Arts
Department of Theatre Arts; University, MS 38677
(601) 232-5816; 232-5968 FAX
Scott McCoy, Head of Directing Program

Degree: M.F.A. **Length of program:** 3 years. **Application deadline:** Mar 31. **Program:** Program is built around a rotating 3-year sequence of styles courses, augmented by studies in history, literature and theory. In addition, the department is production oriented, staging between 10 and 12 productions a year. Directors also receive instruction in single and multi-camera directing techniques, and in directing realistic, nonrealistic and period styles.

University of Montana, Missoula
Drama/Dance Department
Missoula, MT 59812-1058
(406) 243-4481; 243-5726 FAX
Web: http://grizzly.umt.edu/catalog/fadradnc.htm
Randy Bolton, Christine Milodragovich, Co-Chairs

Degree: M.F.A. **Length of program:** 3 years. **Application deadline:** Mar 1. **Program:** Core of the program is a directing sequence promoting a progressive development from the basics of proscenium staging, analysis and the acting process, through advanced conceptual approaches. Paralleling this sequence of courses is a graduated series of directing projects ranging from classroom and laboratory exercises to supported showcases and a final thesis production.

University of North Carolina at Greensboro
Broadcasting/Cinema and Theatre Department
201 Taylor Building; Greensboro, NC 27412
(336) 334-5576; 334-5039 FAX
Web: http://www.uncg.edu/grs/html/drama_mfa.html
Robert C. Hansen, Head of Theatre Department

Degree: M.F.A. in Drama, Directing concentration; M.Ed. in Drama. **Length of program:** 3 years. **Application deadline:** Varies. New students are not admitted every year. **Program:** Designed to develop theatre artists/teachers to work in professional as well as college and university theatre. Students take a core of courses in directing, theatre history, dramatic theory, criticism and dramatic literature. The core is designed to provide a basis for synthesizing the historical, theoretical and literary area for directing a production.

University of Oklahoma
School of Drama
563 Elm Ave, Room 209; Norman, OK 73019-0310
(405) 325-4021; 325-0400 FAX
Dr. Kae Koger, Graduate Liaison

Degree: M.F.A. in Drama, Directing concentration. **Length of program:** 3 years. **Application deadline:** Mar 1. **Program:** Geared toward students who wish to pursue professional careers in educational or commercial theatre. Requires practical directing experience plus a thesis document for successful completion. Graduate students have an opportunity to direct productions in 3 theatre spaces.

University of South Carolina
Department of Theatre, Speech and Dance
Columbia, SC 29208
(803) 777-4288; 777-6669 FAX
E-mail: maulden@garnet.cla.sc.edu
Web: http://www.cla.sc.edu/THSP/index.html
Dennis Maulden, Director of Graduate Studies

Degree: M.F.A. **Length of program:** 3 years. **Application deadline:** Apr 1. **Program:** Directors concentrate on the areas of stage directing; basic scenic, costume and lighting design; communication skills with actors and designers; text analysis and interpretation; theatre history and criticism; and conceptual skills. Students direct at least 4 productions. Study includes a 1-semester internship at the Shakespeare Theatre in Washington D.C.

University of South Dakota
Department of Theatre
414 East Clark St; Vermillion, SD 57069-2390
(605) 677-5418; 677-5073 FAX
Web: http://www.usd.edu/cfa/Theatre/theatre.html
Roberta N. Rude, Department Chair

Degree: M.F.A. in Theatre, Directing concentration. **Length of program:** 3 years. **Application deadline:** Apr 1. **Program:** Prepares the student for a career in the theatre and encourages personal and creative growth. Provides a humanistic education, supplemented by intensive craft training, in which classroom study and practical experience are of equal and complementary value. The department is dedicated to the exploration of new questions, techniques and practices in the theatre.

University of Texas at Austin
Department of Theatre and Dance
Austin, TX 78712-1168
(512) 471-5793; 471-0824 FAX
Web: http://www.utexas.edu/cofa/theatre/
Mary Kay Lutrinter, Graduate Coordinator

Degree: M.F.A. **Length of program:** 3 years. **Application deadline:** Feb 1.
Program: Balances high-quality production/performance work with rigorous academic study where the development of new work, scholarly articles, innovative design and a varied theatre repertory is a high priority. Links to the professional world include a variety of apprenticeship and internship opportunities within the UT Performing Arts Center and regional theatres such as Theatre Under the Stars.

University of Utah
Theatre and Film Department
206 Performing Arts Building; Salt Lake City, UT 84112
(801) 581-6448; 585-6154 FAX
Alex Gelman, Head of M.F.A. Directing

Degree: M.F.A. **Length of program:** 3 years. **Application deadline:** Varies.
Program: Helps each director create a coherent personal concept for productions, and attain a strong craft to bring that vision to fruition. During the program each director presents several productions in a variety of styles.

University of Washington
School of Drama—Professional Director Training Program
Box 353950; Seattle, WA 98195-3950
(206) 543-5140; 543-8512 FAX
E-mail: uwdrama@u.washington.edu
Web: http://artsci.washington.edu/drama/schdram1.html
Mark Harrison, Head, Professional Director Training Program

Degree: M.F.A. **Length of program:** 3 years. **Application deadline:** Jan 15.
Program: Students direct every quarter of their residency, thereby ensuring practical experience in a multiplicity of genres, styles, performance spaces and theatrical collaborations. This work is supported by directing seminars, classes and workshops in the craft. Directors intern either locally, nationally or internationally, as well as direct a mainstage thesis production.

Virginia Commonwealth University
Department of Theatre
Box 842524; Richmond, VA 23284-2524
(804) 828-1514; 828-6741 FAX
James W. Parker, Graduate Studies Director

Degree: M.F.A. **Length of program:** 3 years. **Application deadline:** Varies.
Program: Encompasses both the theoretical and the practical in all aspects of
theatre-related skills. Students are guided in the fundamentals of artistic decision making, as well as in the development of a communicative ability through
which they may participate fully in the creative process of theatre.

Western Illinois University
Department of Theatre
103 Browne Hall; Macomb, IL 61455
(309) 298-1543
Web: http://www.wiu.edu/users/mithea/wiu/
Gene Kozlowski, Department Chairperson

Degree: M.F.A. **Length of program:** 3 years. **Application deadline:** Jan.
Program: Includes one semester of touring theatre during the candidate's second year and one summer of residency in the Summer Music Theatre. The
program is linked to the University's Regional Touring Theatre, which in its
21 years of operation has presented more than 2,700 performances, of more
than 60 different plays, in more than 100 towns and cities in the West-Cen-
tral Illinois region.

Yale University
Yale School of Drama
Box 208325; New Haven, CT 06520-8325
(203) 432-1507
Web: http://www.yale.edu/drama/academics/programs/directing.html
Maria Leveton, Registrar
Stan Wojewodski, Jr., Dean of the Yale School of Drama

Degree: M.F.A. **Length of program:** 3 years. **Application deadline:** Feb 1.
Program: Focuses on developing the skills, craft and attitude to prepare for
the professional theatre, in particular for the demands of repertory and ensemble productions. For the first year, training is closely related to that of actors.
Directors assist on the mainstage productions as well as direct new, realistic
and verse plays.

UNDERGRADUATE COLLEGE AND UNIVERSITY

The following four-year programs culminate in a Bachelor of Fine Arts (B.F.A.) in directing, or theatre arts with a focus on directing. Most colleges, universities and schools that have strong M.F.A. programs have an undergraduate program that emphasizes director-training. Use the above list of M.F.A. director-training programs, as well as the following list, to expand your search.

Arizona State University
Department of Theatre
Box 872002; Tempe, AZ 85287-2002
(602) 965-9432; 965-5351 FAX
Web: http://www.asu.edu/cfa/theatre/index.htm
Marie Fay, Academic Advisor

Degree: B.A. **Length of Program:** 4 years. **Application deadline:** Dec 1.
Program: Offers hands-on theatre training in the new Galvin Playhouse, which houses extensive shops and uniquely equipped rehearsal and instructional spaces. The smaller Lyceum Theatre and the Directing Studio are the venues for student-directed shows. The 20 faculty members provide expertise in all phases of theatrical production.

Coe College
Theatre Arts Department
1220 First Ave N.E.; Cedar Rapids, IA 52402
(319) 399-8624
Dr. Michael Pufall, Head of Department

Degree: B.A. **Length of Program:** 4 years. **Application deadline:** Jan.
Program: Designed to give broad and comprehensive exposure to both intellectual and artistic development in a production-oriented atmosphere. A theatre concentration may also be combined with another discipline to form a collateral concentration. During the third or fourth year, internships are available outside of the college environment.

Lake Erie College
Fine Arts Department
Box 354; 391 West Washington St; Painesville, OH 44077
(216) 639-7856
Web: http://lakeerie.edu/
Paul Gothard, Director

Degree: B.F.A. **Length of Program:** 4 years. **Application deadline:** Five
months before starting date. **Program:** Founded in 1856, Lake Erie College
is a private, co-educational, liberal arts college, which through small classes
and individualized attention creates an environment to support personal development and academic achievement. Emphasis is placed on providing a broad
foundation of theatre training.

Marshall University
Theatre Department
400 Hal Greer Blvd; Huntington, WV 25755-2240
(304) 696-6442; 696-6582 FAX
Web: http://www.marshall.edu/theatre/INDEX.HTMLX
Jeffrey S. Elwell, Department Chair

Degree: B.F.A. **Length of Program:** 4 years. **Application deadline:** Feb 1.
Program: Area of emphasis is on Acting/Directing (with acting emphasized
during the first 2 years of the program). The new 13 million dollar, 3 theatre,
Fine and Performing Arts Center is the home of the Marshall University Theatre and the Department of Theatre/Dance.

Millikin University
Department of Theatre and Dance
1184 West Main St; Decatur, IL 62522
(217) 424-6282; 424-3993 FAX
Web: http://www.millikin.edu/academics/FineArts/theatre/
Barry Pearson, Chair of Department

Degree: B.A. or B.F.A. **Length of Program:** 4 years. **Application deadline:**
Jan 15. **Program:** Employs a contact-intensive approach to teaching and
learning. The focus is on students growing in their personal understanding of
theatre as both art and craft. Performance and the development of artistic
responsibility are emphasized. Degree requirements include courses in acting, history, makeup, stage-craft and play analysis.

New York University
Tisch School for the Arts
Department of Drama, Undergraduate; 721 Broadway, 3rd Floor;
New York, NY 10003-6807
(212) 998-1870
Web: http://www.nyu.edu/tisch/ugdrama.html
Elliot Dee, Director of Recruitment

Degree: B.F.A. **Length of Program:** 4 years. **Application deadline:** Jan.
Program: Students receive their primary professional training from renowned
and respected New York City studios including Playwrights Horizons Theatre School as well as the Experimental Theater Wing. The program admits
approximately 70 students per year.

North Carolina Agricultural and Technical State University
Communication and Theatre Arts
1601 East Market St; Greensboro, NC 27411
(336) 334-7221; 334-7173 FAX
Web: http://www.ncat.edu/theatre/
Miller Lucky Jr., Assistant Professor

Degree: B.A. **Length of Program:** 4 years. **Application deadline:** Nov 1–Jun 1.
Program: Focuses on providing professional and academic attention to individual students. Faculty has experience of working in colleges, universities and
professional venues.

North Carolina School of the Arts
200 Waughtown St; Winston-Salem, NC 27117
(336) 770-3235; 770-3369 FAX
Web: http://www.ncarts.edu/drama/
Robert Beseda, Assistant Dean

Degree: College Arts Diploma or B.F.A. **Length of Program:** 4 years. **Application deadline:** Varies. **Program:** Prepares students for graduate studies in
directing. The course is open to a limited number of students who have had
the equivalent of the first 2 years of actor-training and general studies at the
School of the Arts.

Southern Oregon State College
Department of Theatre Arts
1250 Siskiyou Blvd; Ashland, OR 97520-5099
(503) 552-6346; 552-6429 FAX
Joanna Steinman, Office Coordinator

Degree: B.A. **Length of Program:** 4 years. **Application deadline:** Varies.
Program: Concentration on directing is available to a limited number of students who have demonstrated an unusual degree of maturity, sophistication and aesthetic sensitivity.

Wright State University
Department of Theatre Arts
Dayton, OH 45435
(937) 775-3072
Web: http://www.cola.wright.edu/Dept/TH.html
Dr. W. Stuart McDowell, Chair

Degree: B.A. **Length of Program:** 4 years. **Application deadline:** Varies.
Program: Includes a first and optional second year of the acting program, and 2 years in courses related to directing. The curriculum is especially tailored to meet graduate school requirements, making the student as attractive as possible to major advanced directing programs across the country.

DIRECTING WORKSHOPS

The following workshops have programs specifically geared toward director training. Some are associated with schools or theatres offering experience rather than a formal degree. Mostly all programs listed charge a class fee. Contact the individual program for class dates, times, instructors and cost.

The Barrow Group School
Box 5112; New York, NY 10185
(212) 501-2545; 522-1402 FAX
Nicole Foster, Managing Director

Length of program: Two 10-week directing workshops per/year in the spring and fall. **Application deadline:** Varies. **Approximate cost:** $300 per session.
Program: Four directors are chosen for each workshop through an interview process. Eight actors then join the workshop through an audition process, and

participate in the directors' scenes. At the end of the 10-week session there is a presentation for friends and members of the Barrow Group.

Center Theater Ensemble
The Training Center for Actors, Directors, Playwrights & Singers
1346 West Devon; Chicago, IL 60660
(773) 508-0200
Cindy Birkett, Business Director

Length of program: Classes meet 2 to 3 hours per/week for 8 weeks. **Application deadline:** Varies. **Approximate cost:** $230–$400. **Program:** Designed to expose the emerging director to a variety of styles, techniques and philosophies. Each session is headed by a working professional director focusing on a special aspect of the director's job. Past sessions have focused on adaptation; conceptualization; and Greek, Shakespearean, musical and contemporary work.

Crystal Mountain Theater Institute of the Sangres
Crystal Mountain Center for the Performing Arts
Box 790; Westcliffe, CO 81252
(719) 783-3004
Web: http://jonestheater.com/classes.html
Anne Kimbal Relph, Producing Artistic Director

Length of program: One- to 2-day classes. **Application deadline:** Varies. **Approximate cost:** Varies. **Program:** Summer program offers classes in directing, acting, scene design and dance for early-career artists. Classes are often offered in collaboration with the University of Southern Colorado at Pueblo.

Donna Reed Festival and Workshops for the Performing Arts
1305 Broadway; Denison, IA 51442
(712) 263-3334
E-mail: dreedfpa@pionet.net

Length of program: Jun 14–20. **Application deadline:** Spring. **Approximate cost:** Workshops from $15–$100. Housing $15/night in private homes or $35/night in motels. **Program:** More than 50 workshops on working in theatre and film, including those for working directors.

The Ensemble Studio Theatre Summer Conference
549 West 52nd St; New York, NY 10019
(212) 581-9409, 247-4982
Maria Gabriella, Institute Head

Length of program: Six 1-week (5-day) sessions in Jun/Aug, plus weekend workshops. **Application deadline:** May. **Approximate cost:** $400 for 5-day or $175 for weekend workshops. Six-week residencies also available. Room and board included. **Program:** Five-day or weekend workshops held in Lexington, N.Y., where team works on an existing piece in actor/playwright/director labs. Directing craft sessions are included. Collaboration on new work is encouraged.

HB Studios
120 Bank St; New York, NY 10014
(212) 675-2370
Salem Ludwig, Stephanie Scott, Guest Teachers

Length of program: Varies. **Application deadline:** Varies. **Approximate cost:** Registration fee $35; 1 class $7; 11-week class $77; 19-week class $133. **Program:** Contact studio.

La MaMa Umbria International Workshops
(See Chapter 2: Career Development.)

Lincoln Center Directors Lab
(See Chapter 2: Career Development.)

The New American Theater School at the Women's Projects & Productions
55 West End Ave; New York, NY 10023
(212) 765-1706; 765-2024 FAX
Milan Stitt, Director

Length of program: Six to 8 week sessions. **Application deadline:** Varies. Four sessions per year. **Approximate cost:** $80–$350 per session. **Program:** Year-round program offers directing classes geared toward early- to mid-career directors who are interested in broadening their theatrical focus. Classes include fundamentals, rehearsal techniques, style, playwright/director collaboration, etc. Participants direct workshops of new plays by students.

New Jersey Shakespeare Festival
Summer Professional Training Program
36 Madison Ave; Madison, NJ 07940
(973) 408-3278; 408-3361 FAX
E-mail: njsf@njshakespeare.org
Web: http://www.njshakespeare.org/docs_njsf/title.html
Bonnie J. Monte, Artistic Director

Length of program: Jun 1–Aug 15. **Application deadline:** Mar. **Approximate cost:** Varies. **Program:** Festival offers mixture of Shakespeare and contemporary classics throughout the summer. Internships in directing are available as part of the company, at the F. M. Kirby Shakespeare Theatre. (See Chapter 7: Regional Theatre Opportunities.)

New York Stage and Film's Powerhouse Theater Training Program
Box 225, Vassar College; Poughkeepsie, NY 12604
(914) 437-5473
Web: http://www.vassar.edu/powerhouse
Beth Fargis Lancaster

Length of program: 8 weeks: Jun–Aug. **Application deadline:** Early spring. **Approximate cost:** Tuition, room, board and season theatre tickets are $2,700. **Program:** Held on the 1,000 acre Vassar College campus, this rigorous 8-week training program is for pre-professionals. Visiting master teachers from the professional theatre season, as well as highly respected theatre professionals, teach classes. Collaborative classes with playwrights and actors are available.

Playwrights Horizons Theatre School
440 Lafayette St, 4th Floor; New York, NY 10003
(212) 529-8720; 529-8762 FAX
Web site: http://www.phtschool.org
Michael Lonergan, Administrative Director
Helen R. Cook, Director

Length of program: 6 weeks in summer. **Application deadline:** Jun 1. **Approximate cost:** $2,500 for 40 hour/week course work. **Program:** College credit available through New York University. Classes include storytelling without words, scene work, direction of one-act and full-length plays, and playwright/director collaboration.

Saratoga International Theatre Institute (SITI)
Intensive Summer Training Workshop
Office of the Dean of Special Programs; Skidmore College;
815 North Broadway; Saratoga Springs, NY 12866-1632
(518) 580-5590; 584-7963 FAX
Web site: http:www.skidmore.edu/administration/osp
Anne Bogart, Artistic Director

Length of program: Three weeks. **Application deadline:** Mar 25. **Approximate cost:** $1,025 tuition for credit; $925 for non-credit; $750 room and board; and $30 application fee. **Program:** Open to actors, directors, designers, choreographers, writers and dancers. Fifty-five participants study the Tadashi Suzuki method, with Anne Bogart teaching her Viewpoints technique. Symposia and rehearsals also included. Students work in groups on a project, and each participant is expected to generate a new piece of work presented at the workshop's end.

T. Schreiber Studio
151 West 26th St, 7th Floor; New York, NY 10001
(212) 741-0209; 741-0948 FAX
Terry Schreiber, Director

Length of program: Over a 9-month period, classes are divided into 3, 12-week segments, with classes meeting 1 night a week. **Application deadline:** Varies. **Approximate cost:** $120 per month. **Program:** The Directing Unit offers new directors instruction and experience in the mounting of scenes, one-acts and full-length plays. Every phase of a director's responsibility is explored in a hands-on fashion.

Tisch School for the Arts International Programs
New York University; 721 Broadway, 12th Floor; New York, NY 10003
(212) 998-9175; 995-4610 FAX
Web site: http://www.nyu.edu/tisch/international
Allison Lehr, Program Coordinator

Length of Program: 1 to 3 months. Dates vary. **Application deadline:** Apr 30. **Approximate cost:** Varies. **Program:** Hands-on training that draws on the unique strengths of major European centers. Programs employ faculty from host country, combining training and theory, placing art in a cultural and historical context. Current sites include Dublin, Florence, London and Prague.

CHAPTER 2

CAREER
DEVELOPMENT
OPPORTUNITIES

This chapter focuses on opportunities that allow a director or choreographer to work in the field as either an assistant, observer or working artist. The programs listed are geared toward young directors and choreographers, or more experienced directors and choreographers interested in observing another artist at work. Programs are designed to develop the art and craft of directing and choreographing by offering hands-on experience. Listings are in alphabetical order by title of program, and contain address information and program descriptions. For further information, and to obtain applications to specific programs, contact the organization directly. Also included are Résumé Tips and essays by Julie Hamberg and Sacha Reich, both young directors, who give advice on assistant directing.

DEVELOPMENT OPPORTUNITIES

The following programs offer opportunities for directors and choreographers to hone their craft. Whether you are new to directing or you wish to expand your frame of reference, you may benefit from participation in these programs.

Bailiwick Repertory Director's Festival

Bailiwick Arts Center; 1229 West Belmont; Chicago, IL 60657-3205
(773) 883-1090; 525-3245 FAX
Pat Acerra, Managing Director

The Director's Festival is an annual event that provides an open forum to nurture and showcase the talents of professional directors. It also serves to introduce Chicago audiences to new plays, new playwrights and new performers. Thirty-six directors are selected for each festival. Full productions of each play are mounted. A collaborative effort between writer and director is essential. You may not direct your own work. Productions having previously run in other venues with regular performances of 10 or more showings, are not accepted. Submissions in line with Bailiwick's areas of expertise (classics, new musicals, gay/lesbian, work with deaf actors) are given special attention. Each director receives specific feedback through a post-show discussion, and written evaluations from 3 different directors. There are also pre-performance workshops on subjects such as marketing.

Applications including the director's bio, production concept, full script and royalty arrangement, are due every Apr. The Festival runs from mid-Jul to early Aug. There is a nonrefundable application fee of $10.

Chicago Directors' Forum (CDF)

c/o Effective Theatre; Box 18423; Chicago, IL 60618
(773) 918-8871
E-mail: DirForum@aol.com
Web: http://www.japerformance.com/cdf
Elizabeth Lucas, Chair

The mission of the Chicago Directors' Forum (CDF) is to develop a resource organization for Chicago-area directors. CDF strives to develop a community of stage directors and provide networking opportunities between stage directors and the arts community. CDF facilitates the exchange of ideas and stimulates artistic growth through regular meetings and discussions, Directors' Nights Out, workshops and mentoring programs.

RÉSUMÉ TIPS

The following advice is from an SDC Foundation roundtable discussion entitled "Writing an Effective Résumé."

General Advice

1. Most theatre employers prefer one page résumés.
2. Your most impressive credits should be at the top of the résumé. Chronological listing of credits is typical, but not mandatory. Don't make the reader search for your best credits.
3. Everything about your résumé should make clear what you're after. It is often helpful to have more than one kind of résumé.
4. If you have favorable newspaper or magazine reviews of your work, you may include a quote sheet.
5. Be truthful. It's a small world and most agents and producers are likely to know the play, playwright, producer or theatre company that you have listed.
6. It's a good idea to list the names of playwrights for new and unfamiliar plays. It is also helpful to list theatre companies, producers, directors and choreographers (especially if you were an assistant).
7. List awards and grants you have received near the bottom of the page.
8. Include a section on related experience. For instance, if your résumé is focused on legit theatre as a choreographer, in the related experience section you may mention that you choreographed an industrial, fashion show or video.

Layout

1. If you have work underway, you can highlight it to catch the reader's eye.
2. Create a clean layout, with white space.
3. Help delineate categories and important material with stylistic changes.

Best Time to Send Your Résumé

1. If you have an upcoming production, and would like a particular agent or producer to attend, send your résumé at least two weeks prior to the opening.
2. Send your résumé to a theatre when you know it is selecting talent for the upcoming season.
3. Send your résumé to a theatre, agent or producer anytime another professional has recommended you, especially if that professional is more established than you are.

The Drama League Directors Project
The Drama League of New York; 165 West 46th St, Suite 601;
New York, NY 10036
(212) 302-2100; 302-2554 FAX
E-mail: dlny@echonyc.com
Web: http://www.echonyc.com/~dlny
Roger T. Danforth, Artistic Director

The Drama League Directors Project fosters the development of talented, new directors by providing them entry into the professional theatre, offering practical advice and providing directing experience. A consortium of 24 participating regional theatres across the U.S. offers assistant directing opportunities to Directors Project participants.

There are 4 programs comprising the Directors Project: (1) the Fall Production Program starts with an intensive orientation in New York City, where participants meet with leaders of the artistic community. The directors then complete two assistant directing assignments, one at a regional theatre and one at an Off-Broadway theatre; the program culminates with the participants directing an Equity production in New York City. (2) The Summer Directing Program encompasses an introduction to the New York theatre scene, and workshops and directing opportunities at the Hangar Theatre in Ithaca, NY. (3) The New Directors/New Works program provides rehearsal space and a production stipend for directors and their artistic collaborators, who are then given the opportunity to develop original work. (4) Special Interest Residencies encourage directors to seek out unique experiences that will expand their artistic horizons. The provision of a stipend allows for individually tailored programs, normally lasting 3 to 8 weeks. Applications for all programs begin in the late fall and have a mid-Feb deadline.

The Harold Prince Musical Theatre Program
The Directors Company; 311 West 43rd St, Suite 307; New York, NY 10036
(212) 246-5877; 246-5882 FAX
Michael Parva and Arthur Masella, Artistic Directors

This program focuses on the development and presentation of new musicals. Development sessions take place in New York, culminating in presentations for an invited audience. The Company looks for musical theatre creators as well as directors for this program. The program accepts applications year-round. There is no cost to participants.

AN OLD-FASHIONED APPRENTICESHIP
JULIE HAMBERG, DIRECTOR
NEW YORK CITY

The real reason to assistant direct is to learn from a more established director, whose work you respect. You may want to choose someone whose style you greatly admire, but whose technique is different than yours. If the director is collaborative, you may be able to make a real contribution to the production through your observations or suggestions. Not all directors want, or need, a sounding board, but many appreciate your input. It may take time, however, to establish a relationship in which the director can trust your insights. Over a period of time, the director may become a mentor and friend—or maybe not. Be prepared to keep the relationship on a professional level.

You'll probably be exposed to upper-level casting, how the director works with the actors, the director's approach to staging, his/her communication style with the playwright and designers, how he/she runs technical rehearsals in a large theatre, the director's style of conflict management, etc. You'll probably have the opportunity to work with a casting director, and be exposed to a number of actors with whom you may not be familiar. Assisting may teach you how to take advantage of the preview period—how to handle script changes under the gun, how best to use those rehearsals, or just how much can be accomplished once an audience is put into the equation.

Assisting allows you to get to know the people at the producing organization, possibly opening the door to a future working relationship. You'll be expected to be a liaison to the many different departments involved in the production, and have the opportunity to work with seasoned actors and designers that are of a caliber higher than you could attract at a lower level of production. You may also form friendships with the other assistants working on the project, such as designers, dramaturgs or stage managers, that later turn into collaborations.

Assistant directing can be a poor artist's substitute for graduate school. If the project is large enough, you may get paid, and it may be a way to survive financially, while actually working in the theatre. Look at it as an old-fashioned apprenticeship.

La MaMa Umbria International Workshops
La MaMa E.T.C.; 74A East 4th St; New York, NY 10003
(212) 254-6468; 254-7597 FAX
E-mail: lamamaetc@aol.com
Web: http://www.nytheatre~wire.com
Ellen Stewart, Founder and Artistic Director

La MaMa Umbria International Workshops is a workshop program given by internationally known arts professionals. It offers the opportunity for young theatre artists to study under the guidance of professional artists whose international work, in their specific discipline, is contributing to the shaping of the landscape of the contemporary performing arts. The Workshops are held at The Center of La MaMa Umbria, in the countryside, surrounding the town of Spoleto in central Italy, about two hours from Rome. Participants may reside on-site in the 700-year-old convent that has been transformed into an artists' residence, with rehearsal space, music room, art gallery, archive space and a large outdoor theatre. The internationally acclaimed arts professionals who lead workshops include Andrei Serban, Elisabeth Swados, Eduardo Machado, Tom O'Horgan, Yoshi Oida, Theodora Skipitares, Gerald Thomas, Rodrigo Mendoza and Leon Ingulsrud. Each workshop is priced individually, or you may take all the workshops which run from early-Jul to mid-Aug and live on-site for an all-inclusive price. Applications are accepted at various times, so contact theatre for specific details.

Lincoln Center Directors Lab
Lincoln Center Theater; 150 West 65th St; New York, NY 10023
(212) 501-3100; 873-0761 FAX
Web: http://www.lct/dirlab.html
Anne Cattaneo, Lab Director

The Lab is an interactive forum designed to engage up to 100 emerging directors from the U.S. and abroad in an intensive study of their craft. Designed to foster collaborative relationships among a community of artists, it includes workshops, discussions, master classes, opportunities to direct scenes and short plays with professional actors, and opportunities to observe master directors in rehearsal. The Lab takes place in May/Jun, meeting 6 days per week for 3 weeks. Application deadline is every Mar. There is no charge to participate, and no housing provided.

GOALS FOR ASSISTANT DIRECTING
SACHA REICH, DIRECTOR
NEW YORK CITY

The time commitment in an assistantship is significant, so the arrangement really needs to be worthwhile. It is time that I spend working (with or without pay) on someone else's show. It is time I'm not directing. So it is important to be selective. It is also important to have a strong objective within the assistantship. The more focused I am on what I want to get out of the experience, the more I get.

The goals for entering into an assistantship may be exposure to a specific style of directing, a particular genre of theatre (that I have little experience with), or in order to get acquainted with a particular company from the inside. You may also want to learn a different method of problem solving, or interaction with actors. The opportunities you are seeking rarely exist. They are opportunities you make.

To initiate an assistantship, contact the theatre or director. Do your homework—court them. If the prohibitive factor for the theatre is financial—get a night job, a day job, do what you need to do to make it happen. It is an investment in your artistic future.

Approach the SDC Foundation about their observership/assistantship program. They make exciting director/production matches. It is difficult to be totally passive in the production process of a show, but when you're observing a master, it is still like attending a master class. Sometimes, too, an observership can turn into an assistantship.

Advice to a first timer:
1. Listen
2. Actively observe. Ask yourself: "Why did he do this?"
3. Watch patiently for the answers to emerge.
4. If the director pursues a dialogue with you, speak up. He or she is not looking for a "yes man." You have a brain and a set of eyes for the project.
5. Come prepared by knowing the play well.

New Dramatists
424 West 44th St; New York, NY 10036
(212) 757-6960; 265-4738 FAX
E-mail: newdram@aol.com
Web: http://www.itp.tsoa.nyu.edu/~diana/ndintro.html
Todd London, Artistic Director

Playwright support organization with directing residencies of 3 to 12 months to direct individual readings and workshops. Monthly stipend approximately $500. Send letter of interest and résumé to Todd London of the director program.

Stage Directors and Choreographers (SDC) Foundation
1501 Broadway, Suite 1701; New York, NY 10036
(212) 302-5359; 302-6195 FAX
E-mail: ddstar@compuserve.com
Web: http://www.arts-online.com/sdnc.htm
David Diamond, Executive Director

Programs for career development include the Observership Program, where directors and choreographers have the opportunity to observe the rehearsal process of a more experienced artist. Observers work on Broadway, Off-Broadway and for regional productions. In some cases the observer merely watches the process; in other cases the observer is more of an assistant. To apply, send a letter indicating the type of projects you are interested in observing and your general availability along with a current résumé. You will be contacted when opportunities present themselves. Stipends are available for some projects.

Staged Reading/Works-in-Progress Series is geared toward directors or choreographers who wish to see a project on its feet. Those interested can apply for a slot in the twice-monthly series, which is co-sponsored by Collaborative Arts Project 21. Submit applications to the Foundation with a brief synopsis of the play or performance piece, a statement as to the benefit of the reading at this point in the project's development and a current résumé. Slots are filled several months in advance. Each project is supported with rehearsal space and marketing.

The Networking Group meets on the third Tuesday of each month to share information and solve problems at the Foundation's New York office. Among the kinds of information shared are job opportunities; rehearsal and performance space; referrals of designers, actors, stage managers and tech workers; and other resources. The Networking Group also publishes a Bio Booklet of directors' and choreographers' credits, which is distributed to producers and artistic directors. A Database and a Résumé Notebook housed at the Foundation provide other means for those looking for appropriate directors. (See Chapter 4: Grants, Fellowships; Chapter 5: Service Organizations.)

Sundance Theatre Laboratory
225 Santa Monica Blvd, 8th Floor; Santa Monica, CA 90401
(310) 394-4662; 394-9893 FAX
Philip Himberg, Producing Director

The Sundance Theatre Laboratory is a 3-week-long workshop for directors, playwrights, choreographers, composers and solo performers held at Sundance in Utah. The Lab affords these artists the time and support to develop new theatre texts or to explore new approaches to existing scripts in an environment free from the pressure of production. The Lab is intended to give theatre artists an opportunity to tailor the development process to the project's individual needs, including, but not limited to, text analysis, cold readings, blocking rehearsals, improvisation, music rehearsals, movement-based exploration, choreography and public presentations. The artistic staff is comprised of resource directors, dramaturgs and other artists who are assigned to provide feedback on text and direction. The Theatre Laboratory's mandate includes the support of new work positioned to reach a wide-ranging audience, as well as work that looks at familiar topics using innovative stage techniques, narrative forms and multidisciplinary presentational styles. Sundance looks for original, compelling, human stories that reflect the independent vision of the theatre artist. Projects submitted with a committed director are of particular interest. Also of importance is the Lab's support of the development of projects slated for future production at regional theatres across the nation. There is ongoing support through referral systems which encourage production.

The Laboratory selects up to 10 projects per year. Applications are available every Oct from the Santa Monica office. The deadline for completed applications is mid-Dec with notifications made in Apr. Send letter and résumé.

Theatre LA Job Bank

Theatre LA; 644 South Figueroa St; Los Angeles, CA 90017
(213) 614-0556; 614-0561 FAX
E-mail: theatrela1@aol.com
Web: http://www.theatrela.org
Alisa Fishbach, Executive Director

Theatre LA Job Bank will keep your résumé on file for 6 months for a fee of $20. When producers or others call requesting information about directors or choreographers, they will send or fax a copy of your résumé. It is particularly useful for those looking for internships or first jobs. There is no way to predict availability or positions, and no guarantee that you will be hired.

Women's Theatre Alliance

Box 64446; Chicago, IL 60664-0446
(312) 408-9910; 408-0095 FAX
Director

Women's Theatre Alliance (WTA) is a resource organization of theatre artists from the Chicago area, representing a variety of talents and disciplines, including actors, directors, playwrights, producers, stage managers, technicians, designers and educators. Directors can find opportunities with several of WTA's programs, including Play Developmental Workshops, New Plays Festival, Actors Scene Showcase, and Solo Voices. Membership is $30 annually and includes a monthly newsletter, discounts at WTA events, a hot line with member news, script, résumé and headshot libraries, and discounts at theatres and other businesses.

Women's Work Festival

c/o The Sackett Group; 344 Sackett St; Brooklyn, NY 11231
(718) 643-0919
Dan Haft and Rob Weinstein, Directors

Female directors can apply to participate in this annual festival of one-act plays, usually presented in early spring at a theatre in Manhattan. Application process begins in Jul. Send letter, résumé and description of project.

CHAPTER 3

BOOKS AND PERIODICALS

Much has been written about directing and choreography, including opportunities in the United States and abroad, and how to raise funds for theatrical projects. This chapter contains a list of selected books and periodicals that address such issues, serving as a brief introduction to the many books and periodicals available, ranging from Harold Clurman's classic book On Directing, to the ten-times-per-year American Theatre magazine. To help you locate publications specific to your needs we have subdivided the chapter into the following categories: The Craft and Art of Directing—Books; The Craft and Art of Choreography—Books; Working Abroad; Grants and Funding; Selected Periodicals—Theatre. Listings are in alphabetical order by title. We have also cross-indexed all author and editor names, in case you are searching for a particular author or editor. Under each listing you will find the author or editor's name, publisher, address information, date of publication, number of pages, price and a brief description of content. For more theatre- and dance-related publications, consult the Worldwide Web's http://www.amazon.com, your local book store or library. Please note that all prices were correct at press time, but change frequently.

THE CRAFT AND ART OF DIRECTING — BOOKS

Creative Play Direction, 2nd ed.
Cohen, Robert and Harrop, John
Prentice-Hall; 200 Old Tappan Rd; Old Tappan, NJ 07675
(800) 223-1360; 445-6991 FAX
Web: http://www.prenhall.com
1984. 352 pp, cloth. $67.

College textbook structured around "four concerns of directing the play," including interpretation, composition, acting and style. Advocates directing as a creative rather than imitative art.

Directing Beckett
Oppenheim, Lois
University of Michigan Press; Box 1104; Ann Arbor, MI 48106
(313) 764-4388; (800) 876-1922 FAX
E-mail: um.press@umich.edu
Web: http://www.press.umich.edu
1994. 318 pp, paper. $8.95.

A collection of interviews and essays by directors most closely associated with Samuel Beckett's work in theatres in the U.S. and abroad.

Directing Drama
Miles-Brown, John
Peter Owen (distibuted by Dufour Editions, Inc); Box 7;
Chester Springs, PA 19425
(610) 458-5005; 458-7103 FAX
E-mail: dufour8023.aol.com
Web: http://www.members.aol.com/dufour8023/index.html
1994. 176 pp, paper. $25.

A comprehensive handbook on the direction of stage plays, written specifically for drama students, teachers and amateur theatre groups.

Directing in the Theatre: A Casebook, 2nd ed.
Wills, J. Robert
Scarecrow; 4720 Boston Way; Lanham, MD 20706
(301) 459-3366; 459-2118 FAX
Web: http://www.scarecrowpress.com
1994. 224 pp, cloth. $31.

Presents case studies and discussion questions for each phase of the directing process.

Directing Plays: A Working Professional's Method
Vaughan, Stuart
Longman; 1 Jacob Way; Reading, MA 01867
(800) 358-4566; 367-7198 FAX
Web: http://www.awl.com
1993. 366 pp, cloth. $65.

College textbook containing information on play selection, script analysis, casting, technical concerns, rehearsal strategies, acting and acting styles.

Directing Postmodern Theatre
Whitmore, Jon
University of Michigan Press ; Box 1104; Ann Arbor, MI 48106
(313) 764-4388; (800) 876-1922 FAX
E-mail: um.press@umich.edu
Web: http://www.press.umich.edu
1994. 242 pp, paper. $17.95.

Critical theory and contemporary theatre practice are juxtaposed to explain how performances communicate and how directors can use semiotics as a practical tool in today's theatre.

Directing the Action: Acting and Directing in the Contemporary Theatre
Marowitz, Charles
Applause Books; 211 West 71 St; New York, NY 10023
(212) 496-7511; 721-2856 FAX
1994. 194 pp, paper. $12.95.

Includes meditations on all the sacred precepts of theatre practice, including auditions, casting, design, rehearsal, actor psychology, dramaturgy and the text.

Directors on Directing, 2nd ed.
Cole, Toby and Chinoy, Helen Krich, eds.
Prentice Hall; 200 Old Tappan Rd; Old Tappan, NJ 07675
(800) 223-1360; 445-6991 FAX
Web: http://www.prenhall.com
1986. 480 pp, cloth. $53.

Essays on directing written by masters in the field, from the turn-of-the-century to the present.

The Director's Voice
Bartow, Arthur
Theatre Communications Group; 355 Lexington Ave; New York, NY 10017
(212) 697-5230; 983-4847 FAX
E-mail: custserv@tcg.org
Web: http://www.tcg.org
1988. 360 pp, paper. $16.95.

A collection of interviews with JoAnne Akalaitis, Arvin Brown, René Buch, Martha Clarke, Gordon Davidson, Robert Falls, Zelda Fichandler, Richard Foreman, Adrian Hall, John Hirsch and Mark Lamos.

From Assassins to West Side Story: The Director's Guide to Musical Theatre
Miller, Scott
Heinemann; 361 Hanover St; Portsmouth, NH 08801
(800)793-2154; 847-0938 FAX
Web: http://www.heinemann.com
1996. 239 pp, paper. $19.95.

Miller analyzes sixteen well-known musicals in terms of character, themes, musicality, symbolism and contribution to theatre. Of interest to both directors and fans of musical theatre.

Fundamentals of Play Directing, 5th ed.
Dean, Alexander and Carra, Lawrence
Holt, Rinehart and Winston; 6277 Sea Harbor Dr; Orlando, FL 32887
(800) 225-5425; 269-5232 FAX
E-mail: hbscs.hbschool.com
Web: http://www.harcourtbrace.com
1989. 374 pp, cloth. $61.50.

Dean's college textbook, originally published in 1941, endures a half-century later. Conceived around "Five Fundamental Elements of Directing," including composition, movement, picturization, rhythm and pantomimic dramatization.

The Great Stage Directors: 100 Distinguished Careers of the Theatre
Leiter, Samuel
Facts on File; 11 Penn Plaza, 15th Floor; New York, NY 10001
(212) 967-8800; 967-8107 FAX
E-mail: fof056@mail.infohouse.com
Web: http://www.factsonfile.com
1994. 340 pp, cloth. $35.

Contains biographies and career histories of 100 innovative directors from theatre history and the contemporary stage. Foreword by Simon Callow.

How to Direct a Musical: Broadway—Your Way!
Young, David
Routledge; 7625 Empire Dr; Florence, KY 41022
(800) 634-7064; 248-4724 FAX
Web: http://www.routledge.com
1995. 200 pp, cloth. $25.

Written for anyone who has wanted to direct a musical, this book includes appendices with material for directing youth, teens, disabled, challenged and retired individuals, as well as a section on computer technology related to the production of musicals.

In Contact with the Gods? Directors Talk Theatre
Delgado, Maria M. and Heritage, Paul, eds.
Manchester UP (distributed by St. Martin's Press); 175 Fifth Ave;
New York, NY 10010
(212) 674-5151; (800) 258-2769 FAX
1997. 342 pp, paper. $19.95.

Seventeen contemporary directors reveal insights into their work. This book is international in scope, with special emphasis on directors known for postmodern works. Includes biographical information, critical annotations and a list of each director's production work.

In Other Words: Women Directors Speak
Manfull, Helen
Smith & Kraus; Box 127; Lyme, NH 03768
(603) 643-6431; 643-1831 FAX
E-mail: sandk@sover.net
Web: http://www.smithkrauss.com
1997. 200 pp, paper. $19.95.

Explores the work of British women directors, including Annie Castledine, Phyllida Lloyd, Sue Sutton Mayo, Annabel Arden, Parah Pia Anderson and Katie Mitchell, among others. Features a preface by American director Anne Bogart and an appendix with "Current Thumbnail Biographies."

Making Plays: The Writer-Director Relationship in the Theatre Today
Nelson, Richard and Jones, David
Faber & Faber (distributed by CUP Services); Box 6525; Ithaca, NY 14851
(800) 666-2211; 688-2877 FAX
E-mail: orderbooks@cupserv.org
1995. 165 pp, paper. $13.95.

Chronicles the playwright-director relationship through the rehearsal process of a production of *Misha's Party*. Raises issues about the control of text and meaning in the rehearsal process.

On Directing
Clurman, Harold
Fireside, Simon & Schuster; 200 Old Tappan Rd; Old Tappan, NJ 07675
(800) 223-2336; 445-6991 FAX
Web: http://www.simonsays.com
1997. 299 pp, paper. $15.

Elia Kazan calls this: "The most influential book on direction ever written in this country." Parts I and II cover selection, rehearsal process and audience. Parts III and IV include examples of Clurman's director's notes, script work and letters on past productions.

Play Directing: Analysis, Communication and Style, 4th ed.
Hodge, Francis
Prentice-Hall; 200 Old Tappan Rd; Old Tappan, NJ 07675
(800) 223-1360; 445-6991 FAX
Web: http://www.prenhall.com
1994. 448 pp, cloth. $57.

Hodge's college textbook includes a significant section on script analysis, and is structured to serve both beginners and advanced classes; this book has met demands in the classroom for more than thirty years.

Play Director's Survival Kit.
Rogers, James W. and Rodgers, Wanda C.
Simon & Schuster; 200 Old Tappan Rd; Old Tappan, NJ 07675
(800) 223-2336; 445-6991 FAX
Web: http://www.simonsays.com
1995. 304 pp, paper. $29.50.

A step-by-step guide for beginning stage directors to producing theatre in a school or community setting.

Playing Director: A Handbook for Beginners
Desrochers, Rick
Heinemann; 361 Hanover St; Portsmouth, NH 08801
(800)793-2154; 847-0938 FAX
Web: http://www.heinemann.com
1995. 71 pp, paper. $9.95.

A very basic handbook for those who have never directed before and want to give it a try.

The Production Notebooks: Theatre in Process, Volume 1
Bly, Mark, ed.
Theatre Communications Group; 355 Lexington Ave; New York, NY 10017
(212) 697-5230; 983-4847 FAX
E-mail: custserv@tcg.org
Web: http://www.tcg.org
1996. 280 pp, paper. $16.95.

Four dramaturg production notebooks (from the Guthrie Theatre in Minneapolis, the Alley Theatre in Houston, Crossroads Theatre in New Brunswick and Theatre de la Jeune Lune in Minneapolis) are a testament to the research that can benefit theatrical production. Includes bibliographies for each production and black and white photographs.

Rehearsal Management for Stage Directors
Alberts, David
Heinemann; 361 Hanover St; Portsmouth, NH 08801
(800) 793-2154; 847-0938 FAX
Web: http://www.heinemann.com
1995. 160 pp, paper. $15.95.

From preproduction planning to postproduction evaluation, this is a guide to organizational management, staffing, budgeting, auditioning, casting, developing rehearsal time lines and integrating design and technical elements of a theatrical production.

The Revisionist Stage: American Directors Reinvent the Classics
Green, Amy S.
Cambridge UP; 110 Midland Ave; Port Chester, NY 10573
(800) 872-7423; (914) 937-4712 FAX
E-mail: orders@cup.org
Web: http://www.cup.org
1994. 240 pp, cloth. $59.95.

Green investigates the reworking of classic theatre into works for the modern stage; includes both theoretical and critical histories of revision and studies of specific revisionist works. Special attention is given to Greek and Roman plays, the plays of Shakespeare and Molière, and Peter Sellar's work with opera.

The Semiotic Stage: Prague School Theater Theory
Quinn, M. L.
Peter Lang; 275 Seventh Ave; New York, NY 10001
(800) 770-5264; (212) 647-7707 FAX
Web: http://www.peterlang.com
1995. 166 pp, cloth. $42.95.

For those interested in semiotics and structuralism. The five chapters include Prague School Structuralism, Theory of the Theater, Semiotics of Theatrical Acting, Semiotics of Stage Design, and Semiotics of Theatrical Text.

Sense of Direction: Some Observations on the Art of Directing
Ball, William
Drama Publishers/Quite Specific Media; 260 Fifth Ave, Suite 703;
New York, NY 10001
(212) 725-5377; 725-8506 FAX
E-mail: info@quitespecificmedia.com
Web: http://www.quitespecificmedia.com
1984. 180 pp, paper. $19.95.

A clearly written book that covers the directing process from start to finish, complete with practical examples from Ball's extensive experience. Quickly becoming a staple in the field.

Staging Musical Theatre
Novak, Deborah and Novak, Elaine Adams
Betterway/F & W Publications, Inc; 1507 Dana Ave;
Cincinnati, OH 45207
(513) 531-2222; 531-4744 FAX
1996. 192 pp, paper. $19.99.

Targets producers, directors and choreographers of community theatres and other groups; covers everything from selection and interpretation of musicals to staging and rehearsing musicals, revues and operas.

Staging Premodern Drama
Mitchell, Lee
Greenwood; Greenwood Publishing Group; 82 Post Rd West;
Westport, CT 06881
(203) 226-3571; 222-1502 FAX
Web: http://www.greenwood.com
1984. 237 pp, cloth. $52.95.

Based in part on his course at Northwestern University, Mitchell takes a problem/solution approach to learning how to produce premodern works (excluding Shakespeare).

Take Stage!: How to Direct and Produce a Lesbian Play
Gage, Carolyn
Scarecrow; 4720 Boston Way; Lanham, MD 20706
(301) 459-3366; 459-2118 FAX
Web: http://www.scarecrowpress.com
1997. 205 pp, paper. $38.50.

A collection of essays in response to the author's oppression as a lesbian playwright, producer, director and performer.

Theatre Directory
Theatre Communications Group; 355 Lexington Ave, New York, NY 10017
(212) 697-5230; 983-4847 FAX
E-mail: custserv@tcg.org
Web: http://www.tcg.org
1998. 96 pp, $6.95.

TCG's annually updated directory provides complete contact information for more than 300 not-for-profit professional theatres and more than 50 arts service organizations.

Theatre Games for Rehearsal: A Director's Handbook
Spolin, Viola
Northwestern UP; 625 Colfax St; Evanston, IL 60208
(847) 491-5313; 491-8150 FAX
E-mail: nupress@nwu.edu
1985. 117 pp, paper. $26.95.

The counterpart to Spolin's famous book of acting (improv) exercises, this book provides the director with a variety of exercises that take the cast from the first stage of rehearsal through opening night.

Theatre Profiles 12
Theatre Communications Group; 355 Lexington Ave, New York, NY 10017
(212) 697-5230; 983-4847 FAX
E-mail: custserv@tcg.org
Web: http://www.tcg.org
1996. 240 pp, $22.95.

Contains artistic profiles, production photographs, financial information and repertroire information for the 1993–95 seasons of 257 theatres (the first 11 volumes cover preceding seasons).

Theatrical Directors: A Biographical Dictionary
Frick, John W. and Vallilla, Stephen M., eds.
Greenwood Press; Greenwood Publishing Group;
82 Post Rd West; Westport, CT 06881
(203) 226-3571; 222-1502 FAX
Web: http://www.greenwood.com
1994. 584 pp, cloth. $95.

Contains biographical sketches of nearly 300 individuals distinguished for their stage directing. Emphasis is placed upon artists who have established international reputations, especially those whose work has significantly influenced American theatre.

Upstaging Big Daddy
Donkin, Ellen and Clement, Susan, eds.
University of Michigan Press; Box 1104; Ann Arbor, MI 48106
(313) 764-4388; (800) 876-1922 FAX
E-mail: um.press@umich.edu
Web: http://www.press.umich.edu
1993. 344 pp, paper. $17.95.

Contains essays and interviews by directors, scholars and other theatre specialists. The collection includes essays on African-American theatre, feminist
classics and male directors working on feminist plays, as well as concrete suggestions for directing a variety of plays.

Women Stage Directors Speak: Exploring the Influence of
Gender on Their Work
Daniels, Rebecca
McFarland & Co; Box 611; Jefferson, NC 28640
E-mail: mcfarland.skybest.com
Web: http://www.mcfarlandpub.com
1996. 255 pp, cloth. $29.50.

Daniels (co-founder, Actor's Repertory Theatre, Portland) explores the impact
of gender on the production process. Thirty-five women who are currently
directing give their input on the intricate study of gender.

Working on a New Play
Cohen, Edward M.
Limelight Editions; 118 East 30th St; New York, NY 10016
(212) 532-5525; 532-5526 FAX
E-mail: jjlmlt@idt.net
1988. 216 pp, paper. $13.95.

Explains play development to every participant in the process. Teaches the
basics of the collaborative method, which extends from the writer's first words
through the opening night performance of a new play.

THE CRAFT AND ART OF CHOREOGRAPHY — BOOKS

Choreography: A Basic Approach Using Improvisation, 2nd ed.
Minton, Sandra Cerry
Human Kinetics; Box 5076; Champaign, IL 61825-5076
(800) 747-4457; (217) 351-1549 FAX
Web: http://www.humankinetics.com
1997. 124 pp, paper. $19.95.

Aims to help students cultivate creative choreography and avoid common mistakes.

Choreography Observed
Anderson, Jack, ed.
University of Iowa Press; Publication Order Dept;
2222 Old Highway 218 South; Iowa City, IA 52242-1602
(800) 235-2665; (319) 384-3806 FAX
Web: http://www.uiowa.edu/~uipress
1997. 304 pp, paper. $12.95.

Includes writings from Balanchine, Paul Taylor, Meredith Monk, Arthur Tudor and Alvin Ailey. The essays focus most directly on choreographers and choreography, in order to illuminate the delights and problems of dance and reveal the nature of this art form.

Conversations with Choreographers
Grody, Svetlana and Lister, Dorothy, eds.
Heinemann; 361 Hanover St; Portsmouth, NH 08801
(800)793-2154; 847-0938 FAX
Web: http://www.heinemann.com
1996. 236 pp, paper. $19.95.

Contains a dozen interviews with top choreographers about their technical approach to the craft, including Hermes Pan, Don Saddler, Lee Theodore, Graciela Daniele and Tommy Tune.

Dance Composition, 3rd ed.
Smith-Autard, Jacqueline M.
A & C Black (distributed by Talmon Co.); 89 Fifth Ave, Suite 802;
New York, NY 10003
(212) 352-1770; 352-1772 FAX
E-mail: talmon@infinite.org
1997. 186 pp, paper. $20.95.

Written with dance educators in mind, the book is divided into five sections:
The Material Content (movement and meaning), Methods of Construction
(motif, form, composition), Resource-Based Teaching/Learning of Dance Composition, Standing Back from Process, and Practical Assignments for Students.
Includes the introduction: Dance in Education—Dancing and Making Dances.

Dance Imagery for Technique and Performance
Franklin, E. N.
Human Kinetics; Box 5076; Champaign, IL 61825-5076
(800) 747-4457; (217) 351-1549 FAX
Web: http://www.humankinetics.com
1996. 272 pp, cloth. $24.95.

Includes more than 500 imagery exercises, divided into four sections: Imagery
in Improvisation Exercises, Imagery in Dance Technique Classes, Imagery in
Choreography and Performance, and Rest and Regeneration.

Dancers and Choreographers: A Selected Bibliography
Getz, Leslie
Asphodel Press/Moyer Bell; Kymbolde Way; Wakefield, RI 02879
(888) 789-1945; (401) 789-3793 FAX
E-mail: sales@moyerbell.com
Web: http://www.moyerbell.com
1995. 304 pp, paper. $18.95.

Focuses extensively on ballet and modern dance. Covers the full range of English language dance books and scholarly periodicals in the field from the United
States, Great Britain, Canada and Australia.

Dancers Talking Dance
Lavender, L.
Human Kinetics; Box 5076; Champaign, IL 61825-5076
(800) 747-4457; (217) 351-1549 FAX
Web: http://www.humankinetics.com
1996. 160 pp, paper. $22.

Lavender outlines a five-step approach to critical evaluation of choreography: observation, reflection, discussion, evaluation and recommendations for revision. Although this was intended for classroom use, such a five-step approach may also benefit directors and choreographers in the rehearsal process.

Fight Directing for the Theatre
Suddeth, J. Allen
Heinemann; 361 Hanover St; Portsmouth, NH 08801
(800)793-2154; 847-0938 FAX
Web: http://www.heinemann.com
1996. 344 pp, paper. $39.95.

Covers the "how to" of fight directing, demystifying the process; also suggests a step-by-step method of working with performers and designers in the creation of safe fight choreography.

Hot Jazz and Jazz Dance
Dodge, Roger Pryor, ed.
Oxford University Press; 2001 Evans Rd; Cary, NC 27513
(800) 251-7556; (919) 677-1303 FAX
Web: http://www.oup-usa.org
1995. 384 pp, cloth. $30.

A collection of essays and reviews written between 1929 and 1958 by a ballet, vaudeville and jazz dancer who was also one of America's first great jazz critics.

The Intimate Act of Choreography
Blom, Lynne Anne and Chaplin, Tarlin
University of Pittsburgh (distributed by CUP Services);
Box 6525; Ithaca, NY 14851
(800) 666-2211; 688-2877 FAX
E-mail: orderbooks@cupserv.org
1982. 252 pp, paper. $14.95.

A comprehensive book that covers all aspects of choreography from the most fundamental technique, dealing with time, space and force, to highly sophisticated artistic concerns, including form, style, abstraction, compositional structures and choreographic devises.

A Primer for Choreographers
Ellfeldt, Lois
Waveland Press, Box 400; Prospect Heights, IL 60070
(847) 634-0081; 634-9501 FAX
E-mail: info@waveland.com
1988. 113 pp, paper. $11.95.

Provides answers to the persistent questions of all would-be choreographers, including answers to questions about spatial relationships, visual images, settings, accompaniment and other considerations about composition.

WORKING ABROAD

The following publications are available for a reduced rate if purchased through Arts International (AI), Institute of International Education, 809 United Nations Plaza, New York, NY 10017, (212) 984-5370, (212) 984-5574 FAX; or can be viewed by appointment at the International Theatre Institute (ITI/US), 47 Great Jones St, New York, NY 10012, (212) 254-4141, (212) 254-6814 FAX. (For more information on these two organizations, see Chapter 9: Working Abroad and Foreign Festivals.)

Across the Street Around the World: A Handbook for Cultural Exchange
Williams, Jennifer
British American Arts Association Ltd; 116 Commercial St;
London, England E16NF;
(011) 44-171-247-5385, 44-171-247-5256
1996. Retail: $14.95; AI: $12.95.

This handbook provides useful information for those starting out in the field of cultural exchange. It is geared toward artists, parents, teachers, community workers and producers who are beginning international projects. Chapters include information on planning, fundraising, evaluation and international contacts. A recommended reading list is included.

Cultural Organizations in Southeast Asia
Lindsay, Jennifer
Australia Council; 181 Lawson St; Redfern, Sydney, Australia NSW 2012;
Box 788; Strawberry Hills, Sydney, Australia NSW 2012;
(011) 02-950-9000; 02-950-9111 FAX
1994. AI: $20.

This guide for artists, performers and cultural workers interested in Southeast Asia is not a strict directory on performing arts agencies. Instead it is a survey describing the framework for culture in Vietnam and 6 countries of the Association of Southeast Asia. The guide concentrates on the administrative structure for cultures, visual arts, museums, performing arts and libraries. It includes information on Vietnam, the Philippines, Thailand, Malasia, Singapore, Brunei and Indonesia.

Guide to Funding for International and Foreign Programs
The Foundation Center; 79 Fifth Ave, 8th Floor;
New York, NY 10003-3076;
(212) 620-4230; 691-1828 FAX
Web: http://www.fdncenter.org
1996. Retail: $115; AI: $98.

This guide is designed to help those seeking grants from U.S. corporations and foundations for international and foreign projects. Listings contain contact information, foundation type, financial data, purpose and activities, fields of interest, types of support, limitations, publications and administrative staffing.

Money for International Exchange in the Arts,
A Comprehensive Resource Guide
ACA Books; Arts International; 809 United Nations Plaza;
New York, NY 10017
(212) 984-5370; 984-5574 FAX
1992. Retail: $14.95; AI: $10.95.

This guide includes profiles of 160 organizations that offer information and technical assistance; organize exchange programs, exhibitions and presentations; or provide grants, fellowships and awards to artists and arts organizations. Each entry lists contact names and addresses, a brief profile and a summary of guidelines and areas of interest, and whether grants are awarded to individuals and/or groups.

Music, Opera, Dance and Drama in Asia,
the Pacific, and North America (MOD)
Arts Publishing International Ltd; 4 Assam St; London England E17QS;
(011) 44-171-247-0066; 44-171-247-6868 FAX
E-mail: editorial@api.co.uk
1995. AI: $50.

The MOD guide focuses on the performing arts of the U.S., Canada, Mexico, Cuba, Australia, New Zealand, Japan, Hong Kong, Taiwan, Korea, Indonesia, Singapore and the Philippines. The MOD guide includes state and local information on funding agencies throughout these regions.

Performing Arts Year Book for Europe (PAYE) 1996
Arts Publishing International Ltd; 4 Assam St; London, England E17QS;
(011) 44-171-247-0066; 44-171-247-6868 FAX
E-mail: editorial@api.co.uk
1996. Retail: $75; AI: $65.

The PAYE directory lists the names and contact details for over 14,000 arts
organizations in more than 50 European countries. Although the guide focuses primarily on the work of large to moderately sized professional companies,
it does list notable companies that operate on a smaller scale. Also included
are specialization, number of performances, touring information and articles
by directors and managers of festivals.

GRANTS AND FUNDING

*The following publications contain information on grants, awards and fellowships for
all fields in the arts and humanities. This list does not include all such publications.
For more information on books and periodicals addressing available grants, you may
contact or visit The Foundation Center, 79 Fifth Ave, 8th Floor, New York, NY
10003, (212) 620-4230. (Also see Chapter 4: Grants, Fellowships.)*

*Arts Funding: A Report on Foundation and
Corporate Grant Making Trends*
The Foundation Center; 79 Fifth Ave, 8th Floor; New York, NY 10003;
(212) 620-4230; 691-1828 FAX
Web: http://www.fdncenter.org
1993. 187 pp, paper. $40.

Provides a framework for understanding trends in foundation funding for arts
and culture. Analyzes grants awarded in the 1980s, and includes profiles of
more than 60 top foundation and corporate grantmakers.

Arts Funding Revisited
The Foundation Center; 79 Fifth Ave, 8th Floor; New York, NY 10003;
(212) 620-4230; 691-1828 FAX
Web: http://www.fdncenter.org
1995. 31 pp, paper. $14.95.

Focuses on grantmaking in 1992, updating their original study (above listed
publication) by 3 years. Analyzes more than 9,500 awarded grants, by major
U.S. arts and culture grantmakers.

ArtSEARCH
Theatre Communications Group; 355 Lexington Ave; New York, NY 10017;
(212) 697-5230; 983-4847 FAX
E-mail: orders@tcg.org
Web: http://www.tcg.org
Individual subscription (with E-mail): $64; Institution subscription
(with E-mail): $90. Bimonthly.

The "Career Development" section of *ArtSEARCH*, while comprised mostly
of non-paying internships, also lists fellowships, graduate assistantships, residencies and other sources of short- and long-term employment.

Directory of Grants in the Humanities
ORYX Press; Box 33889; Phoenix AZ 85067-3889
(800) 279-6799; 279-4663 FAX
E-mail: info@oryxpress.com
Web: http://www.oryxpress.com/cpyrt.htm
1998/99. 786 pp, paper. $84.50.

This guide to grants and other funding for the humanities includes more than
3,400 listings with details necessary to submit proposals to the right people at
the right time. Programs listed are for individuals and organizations that are
sponsored by corporations, foundations, professional associations, as well as
those funded by NEA, NEH and state and local arts and humanities councils.
Information includes funding for awards, artist residencies, arts in education
and much more.

The Foundation Center's Guide to Proposal Writing
Geever, Jane C. and McNeill, Patricia, eds.
The Foundation Center; 79 Fifth Ave, 8th Floor; New York, NY 10003;
(212) 620-4230; 691-1828 FAX
Web: http://www.fdncenter.org
1997. 191 pp, paper. $34.95.

A comprehensive manual on the basic and finer points of writing proposals.
Contains interviews with people who review proposals; also furnishes "insid-
er information" from grantmakers who advise on the best proposal strategies.
This current edition guides the reader through the entire grantwriting process,
from pre-proposal planning, to the writing itself, to the post-grant follow-up.

Foundation Grants to Individuals
The Foundation Center; 79 Fifth Ave, 8th Floor; New York, NY 10003
(212) 620-4230; 691-1828 FAX
Web: http://www.fdncenter.org
1997. 630 pp, paper. $65.

Devoted exclusively to foundation funding opportunities for individual
grantseekers. Features more than 3,300 entries with contact information,
financial data, application information and program descriptions. Includes 6
indexes to help users target prospective grants by subject area, types of support, geographic area, sponsoring company, educational institution and grant-
maker names.

Guide to U.S. Foundations, Their Trustees, Officers and Donors
The Foundation Center; 79 Fifth Ave, 8th Floor; New York, NY 10003
(212) 620-4230; 691-1828 FAX
Web: http://www.fdncenter.org
1997. 2 vols. 4,235 pp, paper. $225.

This 2-volume reference collection is the only published source of data on all
active grantmaking foundations. It provides information on more than 40,000
foundations and features a master list of the decision makers who direct America's foundations.

National Guide to Funding in Arts & Culture
The Foundation Center; 79 Fifth Ave, 8th Floor; New York, NY 10003
(212) 620-4230; 691-1828 FAX
Web: http://www.fdncenter.org
1996. 1,138 pp, paper. $145.

Provides essential facts on more than 4,200 foundations, corporate direct-giv-
ing programs and public charities, each with a history of awarded grant dollars to arts and culture-related projects and organizations.

SELECTED PERIODICALS — THEATRE

American Theatre
Theatre Communications Group ; 355 Lexington Ave; New York, NY 10017
(212) 697-5230; 983-4847 FAX
E-mail: at@tcg.org
Web: http://www.tcg.org
Editor: O'Quinn, Jim
Frequency: 10 times/year. **Book reviews:** Yes. **Performance reviews:** Yes.
Subscription: $35/year. **Single issue:** $4.95.

Addresses theatre nationwide, but focuses primarily on American not-for-profit
professional theatres. Features complete new scripts, a season preview issue and
Theatre Facts: a statistical report on theatre finance, production and audience.

Asian Theatre Journal
University of Hawaii Press; 2840 Kolowalu St; Honolulu, HI 96822-1888
(808) 956-8697; 988-6833 FAX
E-mail: aludeman@hawaii.edu
Editor: Leiter, Samuel
Frequency: Semiannual. **Book reviews:** Yes. **Performance reviews:** Yes.
Subscription: $22/year. **Single issue:** $22.

A publication of the Association for Asian Performance (ATHE affiliate), this
journal includes research on both traditional and current Asian theatrical productions, as well as the relations between Eastern and Western theatre.

Back Stage
1515 Broadway; New York, NY 10036
(212) 764-7300; 536-5318 FAX
E-mail: bstage@bstage.com
Web: http://www.backstage.com
Editor: Eaker, Sherry
Frequency: Weekly. **Book reviews:** Yes. **Performance reviews:** Yes.
Subscription: $84/year.

Weekly newspaper includes theatre news, theatre reviews, features, casting
notices and job listings. The focus is on actors both in New York and regionally, but there are frequent articles of interest to directors and choreographers,
including periodic resource guides.

Back Stage West/Dramalogue
2035 Westwood Blvd, #210; Los Angeles, CA 90025
(310) 474-6161; 474-3668 FAX
West Coast Editor: Kendt, Rob

West coast version of *Back Stage* with major focus on Los Angeles area.

The Brecht Yearbook
Brecht Society of America; 59 South New St; Dover, DE 19904-3230
(302) 734-3740
Editor: Fuegi, John
Frequency: Annual. **Book reviews:** Yes. **Performance reviews:** No.
Subscription: $35/year.

Articles are published in English, with German and French synopses. Each issue has a specific focus, such as "Brecht and Women" or "Brecht and Socialism." The editors encourage contributory essays on any aspect of Brechtian study.

Comparative Drama
Department of English, Western Michigan University;
Medieval Institute Publications; Kalamazoo, MI 49008
(616) 387-8753; 387-8750 FAX
Editors: Davidson, Clifford and Stoupe, John H.
Frequency: Quarterly. **Book reviews:** Yes. **Performance reviews:** No.
Subscription: $18/year. **Single issue:** $10.

This scholarly publication addresses an international and interdisciplinary audience. Articles focus on the literary study of dramatic works.

Dramatics
Educational Theatre Association; 3368 Central Pkwy;
Cincinnati, OH 45225
(513) 559-1996; 559-0012 FAX
E-mail: pubs@one.net
Web: http://www.etassoc.org
Editor: Corathers, Don
Frequency: 9 times/year. **Book reviews:** Yes. **Performance reviews:** No.
Subscription: $18/year (with membership). **Single issue:** $2.50.

Geared toward theatre for high school students, this magazine includes information on many aspects of theatre, including summer and college theatre directories, and theatre careers; also publishes new plays.

InTheatre
Parker Publishing & Communications; 1501 Broadway, Suite 2605;
New York, NY 10036
(212) 719-9777; 719-4877 FAX
Editor: Henderson, Kathy
Frequency: Weekly. **Book reviews:** No. **Performance reviews:** Yes.
Subscription: $78/year. **Single issue:** $3.

The main focus of this publication is current theatre in New York, but correspondents around the country also contribute. In addition to theatre gossip, theatre news, NYC listings of what's playing and reviews, the magazine covers CD releases (theatre-related), and includes a section called "Class Acts," with tips for teaching.

The Journal for Stage Directors and Choreographers
Stage Directors and Choreographers Foundation;
1501 Broadway, Suite 1701; New York, NY 10036
(212) 302-5359; 302-6195 FAX
E-mail: ddstar@compuserve.com
Web: http://www.arts-online.com/sdnc.htm
Editor: O'Quinn, Jim
Frequency: Semiannual. **Book reviews:** Yes. **Performance reviews:** No.
Subscription: $18/year. **Single issue:** $10.

Includes interviews with top professionals in the field, along with resource guides and updates on the SDC Foundation. Each issue has a special topic.

Modern Drama
Graduate Center for Study of Drama; University of Toronto Press;
5201 Dufferin St; North York, Ontario, Canada M3H 5T8
(416) 667-7791; 667-7832 FAX
E-mail: journals@utpress.utoronto.ca
Editor: Howard, P.
Frequency: Quarterly. **Book reviews:** Yes. **Performance reviews:** No.
Subscription: $28/year. **Single issue:** $8.

Focus of the journal is to aid in the teaching of drama, post-Ibsen. One special-topic issue is published annually.

Performing Arts Journal
Johns Hopkins UP; 2715 North Charles St; Baltimore, MD 21218-4363
(410) 516-6987; 516-6968 FAX
Web: http://www.press.jhu.edu/journals/performing_arts_journal
Editors: Marranca, Bonnie and Dasgupta, Gautam
Frequency: 3 times/year. **Book reviews:** Yes. **Performance reviews:** Yes.
Subscription: $24/year. **Single issue:** $8.50.

This journal includes critical essays on the performing arts both in this country and abroad.

PerformInk
PerformInk, Inc.; 3223 North Sheffield; Chicago, IL 60657
(773) 296-4600; 296-4621 FAX
E-mail: performink@aol.com/knowitalls@performink.com
Editor: Bernardi-Reis, Nicole
Frequency: Biweekly. **Book reviews:** No. **Performance reviews:** Yes.
Subscription: $27.95/year. **Single issue:** $2.

Addresses national theatre, but focuses primarily on theatre in the Chicago area. Features theatre-related articles and information on classes, workshops and auditions in the Chicago area.

Playbill: The National Theatre Magazine
Playbill; 52 Vanderbilt Ave; New York, NY 10017
(212) 557-5757; 682-2932 FAX
Web: http://www.playbill.com
Editor: Samelson, Judy
Frequency: Monthly. **Book reviews:** No. **Performance reviews:** No.
Subscription: $24/year. **Single issue:** $2.50.

Contains news, information and program notes, primarily about theatre on and Off-Broadway.

Show Music
Goodspeed Opera House Foundation; Box 466;
East Haddam, CT 06423-0466
(860) 873-8664
Editor: Preeo, Max
Frequency: Quarterly. **Book reviews:** Yes. **Performance reviews:** Yes.
Subscription: $19/year. **Single issue:** $6.

A musical theatre magazine with new cast releases, video reviews, production reviews (both in the U.S. and abroad) and feature articles on musical theatre. Often publishes photographs that are not seen elsewhere.

TCI (Theatre Crafts International)
Intertec Publishing Corporation; 32 West 18th St;
New York, NY 10011-4612
(212) 229-2965; 229-2084 FAX
Editor: Johnson, David
Frequency: 11 times/year. **Book reviews:** No. **Performance reviews:** No.
Subscription: $45. **Single issue:** $5.

A well-illustrated publication dedicated to technical, design and managerial aspects of the entertainment industry.

T D & T
(formerly *Theatre Design and Technology*)
USITT; 6443 Ridings Rd; Syracuse, NY 13206
(800) 93-USITT; (315) 463-6525 FAX
Web: http://www.culturenet.com/usitt
Editor: Rodger, David
Frequency: Quarterly. **Book reviews:** Yes. **Performance reviews:** No.
Subscription: $80/year (including membership). **Single issue:** $9
(nonmember), $6 (member).

Published under the auspices of the United States Institute for Theatre Technology, this periodical addresses theatrical designers and technicians.

TDR
MIT Press, for Tisch School for the Arts, New York University;
721 Broadway, Room 626; New York, NY 10003-6807
(212) 998-1626; 995-4571 FAX
E-mail: tdr@nyc.edu
E-mail: journals-orders@mit.edu
Editor: Schechner, Richard
Frequency: Quarterly. **Book reviews:** Yes. **Performance reviews:** Yes.
Subscription: $35/year. **Single issue:** $10.

Scholarly in tone, this journal includes a wide range of performance-related essays on such subjects as performance theory, social sciences, literary theory, feminism, semiotics, history, philosophy, linguistics and aesthetics.

Text and Performance Quarterly (TPQ)
National Communication Association; 5105 Backlick Rd, Building E;
Annandale, VA 22003
(703) 750-0533; 914-9471 FAX
Web: http://www.natcom.org
Editor: Hamera, Judith
Frequency: Quarterly. **Book reviews:** Yes. **Performance reviews:** No.
Subscription: $110/year. **Single issue:** $28.

Useful to those interested in the interdisciplinary aspects of theatre, especially as they relate to the communications process. Includes a substantial section of signed book reviews.

Theatre Journal
Johns Hopkins UP; Journal Publishing Division,
Box 19966; Baltimore, MD 21211
(410) 516-6987; 516-6968 FAX
Editor: Kruger, Loren and Bennett, Susan
E-mail: jlorder@jhunix.hcf.jhu.edu
Web: http://muse.jhu.edu/journals/theatre_journal/
Frequency: Quarterly. **Book reviews:** Yes. **Performance reviews:** Yes.
Subscription: $31/year. **Single issue** $8.

This journal is designed to provide an outlet for criticism and scholarship in theatre. Articles cover a wide variety of topics and are international in scope. One special feature is an annual list of doctoral projects in progress.

Theater Magazine
Yale School of Drama; 222 York St; New Haven, CT 06520
(203) 432-9664; 432-8336 FAX
Editor: Munk, Erika
Frequency: 3 times/year. **Book reviews:** Yes. **Performance reviews:** Yes.
Subscription: $22/year. **Single issue:** $8.

Geared toward contemporary plays and performances; issues include interviews, reviews and essays.

Theatre Notebook
The Society for Theatre Research; c/o The Theatre Museum;
1E Tavistock St; London, England WC2E 7PA;
Editor: Jackson, Russell
Frequency: 3 times/year. **Book reviews:** Yes. **Performance reviews:** No.
Subscription: $30. **Single issue:** Price not available.

Subtitled "A Journal of the History and Technique of the British Theatre," in addition to historical essays and book reviews, this journal features a "Notes and Queries" section and a list of recent acquisitions at The Theatre Museum.

Theatre Record
Ian Herbert; 305 Whitton Dene; Isleworth, Middlesex, England TW7 7NE;
44-181-892-6087; 44-181-893-9677 FAX
Editor: Herbert, Ian
Frequency: Biweekly. **Book reviews:** No. **Performance reviews:** Yes.
Subscription: £140/year (Europe), £170/year (all other locations).
Single issue: Price not available.

Formerly entitled *The London Theatre Record*, this publication serves as a "continuing chronicle of the English stage." Composed of reviews of current productions from London and other regional (English) theatres, reprinted from newspapers and other periodicals. Includes an annual index.

Theatre Research International
Oxford UP for the International Federation for Theatre Research;
2001 Evans Rd; Cary, NC 27513
(800) 852-7323; (919) 677-1714 FAX
E-mail: jnl.info@oup.co.uk
Web: http://www.oup.co.uk/journals
Editor: Schumacher, Claude
Frequency: 3 times/year. **Book reviews:** Yes. **Performance reviews:** No.
Subscription: £69/year (England), £131/year (all other locations).
Single Issue: Price not available.
A journal of critical, historical and theoretical research. Approximately two-thirds of each journal is devoted to book reviews.

Theatre Studies
Ohio State University, Lawrence and Lee Theatre Research Institute;
1800 Cannon Dr; 1430 Lincoln Tower; Columbus, OH 43210-1209
(614) 292-6614
Editor: Kattelman, Beth
Frequency: Annual. **Book reviews:** Yes. **Performance reviews:** No.
Subscription: $10/year. **Single issue:** $8.

Publishes papers of graduate students from American universities with Ph.D. programs. Subject areas include theatre history, criticism, theory, performance studies and dramatic literature.

Theatre Topics
Johns Hopkins UP for the Association for Theatre in Higher Education;
2715 North Charles St; Baltimore, MD 21218-4363;
(410) 516-6964; 516-6968 FAX
Web: http://muse.jhu.edu/journals/theatre%5Ftopics
Editor: Burgoyne, Suzanne
Frequency: Semiannual. **Book reviews:** No. **Performance reviews:** No.
Subscription: $20/year. **Single issue:** $11.

Publishes articles in dramaturgy, performance studies and theatre pedagogy. Written for a general audience of theatre practitioners and educators.

CHAPTER 4

GRANTS
FELLOWSHIPS
AND STATE ARTS
COUNCILS

When beginning a search for money to support a project, the best place to start is the Foundation Center in your area, or a local library that carries Foundation Center publications. The Center offers classes and information on funding and grants, which are available to individuals and arts organizations. For further information about the Center, see their listing following this introduction.

This chapter begins with an essay by Greg McCaslin, Program Director for the Center for Arts Education in New York City, who gives advice on grantwriting. Following are grants and fellowships available to directors and choreographers. These listings are in alphabetical order, by title of program, and include address information and a brief description of the grant or fellowship offered.

Since most state arts councils or agencies offer funding for special projects or programs (predominately to residents of the given state), we have included them here. We have listed contact information for each state agency in alphabetical order by state. For more information on programs (too numerous to publish here) offered by a particular state, we suggest you refer to their Web Sites or contact them directly.

The last section of this chapter contains regional arts organizations, which generally serve more than one state, and offer grants and fellowships to residents of all states under their auspices. We've listed these organizations in alphabetical order by title, and have included address information, a brief description of services and a list of states that each one serves.

Also of great help are the following publications listed in our Books and Periodicals Chapter: Arts Funding: A Report on Foundation and Corporate Grant Making Trends; Arts Funding Revisited; ArtSEARCH; Directory of Grants in the Humanities; The Foundation Center's Guide to Proposal Writing; Foundation Grants to Individuals; Guide to U.S. Foundations, Their Trustees, Officers and Donors; National Guide to Funding in Arts & Culture.

The following CD-ROMs can be borrowed from The Foundation Center or through college libraries: BoardLink lists board members for more than 13,000 corporations and foundations; The Chronicle Guide to Grants provides information about grantmakers and their recipients; InfoTax includes tax exempt organizations; ORYX Grants Database contains descriptive listings for more than 8,600 grants; Philanthropy Digest offers abstracts about philanthropy-related news articles; and Prospector's Choice provides detailed information for more than 11,000 corporate and foundation grantmakers.

THE FOUNDATION CENTER

National Collections
79 Fifth Ave, 8th Floor; New York, NY 10003-3076
(212) 620-4230; 691-1828 FAX
Web: http://www.fdncenter.org
Sarah Collins, Director
and
1001 Connecticut Ave, NW; Washington, D.C. 20036-5588
(202) 331-1400; 331-1739 FAX
Patricia E. Pasqual, Director

Field Offices
312 Sutter St, Room 312; San Francisco, CA 94108-4314
(415) 397-0902; 397-7670 FAX
Nadya Disend, Director
and
1422 Euclid Ave, Suite 1356; Cleveland, OH 44115-2001
(216) 861-1933; 861-1936 FAX
Mary Crehore, Director
and
50 Hurt Plaza, Suite 150; Atlanta, GA 30303-2914
(404) 880-0094; 880-0087 FAX
Pattie J. Johnson, Director

The Foundation Center is a not-for-profit service organization established in 1956. It's mission is to foster public understanding of the foundation field by collecting, organizing, analyzing and disseminating information on foundations, corporate giving and related subjects. Its audiences include grantseekers, grantmakers, researchers, policymakers, the media and the general public. The Center maintains an electronic database with information on virtually every active grantmaking foundation in the U.S. While operating 5 professionally staffed libraries, which are open to the public free of charge, the Center supports a nationwide network of more than 200 Cooperating Collections that offer local access to a core collection of Center materials, and publishes books (See Chapter 3: Books and Periodicals), ranging from comprehensive reference works to basic primers on fundraising and not-for-profit management. The Center conducts research on the growth of the foundation field and trends in foundation support of the not-for-profit sector; provides information and resources electronically, via the World Wide Web, CD-ROMs and DIALOG; and offers educational programs on the funding research process, proposal writing, grantmakers and their giving, and related topics.

WRITING GRANT PROPOSALS
GREG McCASLIN, PROGRAM DIRECTOR
CENTER FOR ARTS EDUCATION, NEW YORK CITY

Obtaining funding for the arts requires research, the development of relationships and the preparation of proposals. I'm going to focus on the last point only. Here are some points to keep in mind when writing a grant proposal:

1. Follow the funder's directions. Be clear and concise.
2. Proposal writing is persuasive writing.
3. A proposal writing workshop offered by organizations, such as The Foundation Center or the Support Center for Nonprofit Management (See Chapter 5: Service Organizations) can be very helpful.
4. Understand the definition of a grant proposal: a document that requests a specific amount of money, to be used in a specific way, over a specific period of time, to achieve specific objectives that meet specific needs.
5. Include a *brief* cover letter with your proposal.
6. A proposal/narrative usually consists of the following parts:
   a) a brief summary of the project;
   b) background information establishing your credibility (previous work that you have done, where you have worked, etc.);
   c) the problem/need that your project addresses;
   d) objectives (or measurable outcomes);
   e) your methods (or what you plan to do with the money);
   f) a description of how you will evaluate your project and determine your success in achieving your objectives;
   g) any additional support you have in place for the project (additional funders, donated services, potential for earned income, etc.);
   h) a proposed budget;
   i) any relevant supporting materials (résumés, reviews of previous work, etc.).

GRANTS AND FELLOWSHIPS

The Allen Lee Hughes Fellowship
Arena Stage; 1101 Sixth St, SW; Washington, DC 20024
(202) 554-9066; 488-4056 FAX
E-mail: arenastg@shirenet.com
Web: http://www.arenastage.org
A. Lorraine Robinson, Fellows and Intern Program Coordinator

Arena Stage offers The Allen Lee Hughes Directing Fellowship to individuals of color. The Fellows participate in Arena Stage activities and informal seminars for one season (Sept–Jun, approximately 40 weeks) with a stipend of $10,000 (does not include housing or transportation). The application deadline is Apr 1.

Bush Artist Fellowship
The Bush Foundation; E-900 First National Bank Building;
332 Minnesota St; St. Paul, MN 55101
(651) 227-5222, (800) 605-7315; (651) 297-6485 FAX
E-mail: julie@bushfound.org
Julie Dalgleish, Program Director

The Bush Artist Fellowship provides artists living in Minnesota, North Dakota, South Dakota or 26 counties of northwestern Wisconsin with financial support, which enables them to further their work and contribution to their communities. Fifteen Fellows at any stage in their career may take time for solitary work, reflection, to engage in collaborative community projects or to embark on travel and research. Awards are made in 6 categories which rotate on a 2-year cycle: Choreography/Multimedia/Performance Art; Visual Arts (2-D and 3-D); Literature; Music Composition; Scriptworks; Film/Video. Each Fellow receives $40,000 for 12–18-month period. Application deadline is every Oct.

Headlands Center for the Arts Residencies
Headlands Center for the Arts; 944 Fort Barry; Sausalito, CA 94965
(415) 331-2787; 331-3857 FAX
E-mail: headlands@artswire.org
Kathryn Reasoner, Executive Director

The mission of the program is to provide a laboratory for the development of new work and a place for the exchange of ideas among a variety of cultural and professional disciplines; and to foster creative investigations of the interdependence between human and natural systems.

Feb–Nov residencies are available to California, North Carolina and Ohio residents only, with a stipend of $500/per month for those living on premises, and $2,500/per month for California residents not living on premises.

Jean Dalrymple Awards

c/o American Theatre of Actors; 314 West 54th St; New York, NY 10019
(212) 581-3044
James Jennings, Artistic Director of American Theatre of Actors

The Jean Dalrymple Awards were founded to recognize and encourage new, talented directors, playwrights and actors. There is no application process.

Jerome Foundation Travel and Study Grant Program

Jerome Foundation; 125 Park Square Court; 400 Sibley St;
St. Paul, MN 55101
(612) 224-9431; 224-3439 FAX
E-mail: info@jeromefdn.org
Web: http://www.jeromefdn.org
Vickie Benson, Program Officer

The Jerome Foundation Travel and Study Grant Program supports study and travel during significant periods of professional development for individuals working in the not-for-profit communities of dance, theatre, literature, media arts, music and the visual arts. Grants of up to $5,000 are available to residents of the Twin Cities metropolitan and greater Minnesota regions. Application deadline is every spring.

Kentucky Foundation for Women, Inc. Grants Program

Kentucky Foundation for Women, Inc.; 1215 Heyburn Bldg;
332 West Broadway; Louisville, KY 40202
(502) 562- 0045; 561-0420 FAX
E-mail: kfw@kfw.org
Web: http://www.kf.org
Pat Buster, Grants Administrator

Grants are available to feminist artists living or working in Kentucky, with the goal of improving the status of women in the arts and bringing about social change through the arts. Similar works with strong Kentucky ties by non-residents are considered. Work must be significant in its development of feminist theatre and avoid stereotypes. The foundation has a special interest in street theatre, collaborative theatre, pageants, puppetry and festivals of work by women without "a hierarchy of stars." Thirty-one grants totaling $121,670, ranging from $1,000 to $15,000 each, are available. Application deadline is Oct 1.

Manhattan Community Arts Fund
c/o Lower Manhattan Cultural Council; 5 World Trade Center, Suite 9235;
New York, NY 10048
(212) 432-0900

The Lower Manhattan Cultural Council is a cultural service organization dedicated to supporting artists through programs and projects which promote understanding, respect and a joyful appreciation of a wide area of artists and art forms. The Manhattan Community Arts Fund's goal is to increase support to community-based emerging individual artists and groups of artists by providing them with government funds to which they do not normally have access. Grants of up to $2,000 are available to Manhattan-based individual artists, individual groups of artists applying through a fiscal conduit, and Manhattan-based arts groups that are not currently receiving support from the Department of Cultural Affairs (DCA) or the New York State Council on the Arts (NYSCA).

National Endowment for the Arts
(See Chapter 5: Service Organizations.)

Northwood University Alden B. Dow Creativity Center Residency
Northwood University Alden B. Dow Creativity Center; 3225 Cook Rd;
Midland, MI 48640-2398
(517) 837-4478; 837-4468 FAX

The Creativity Center welcomes applications from all disciplines and areas of interest including the arts, sciences and humanities. The award includes travel to and from Midland for the 10-week residency (mid-Jun to mid-Aug); individual use of a large, furnished apartment in a wooded environment; a per diem; and a stipend of $750/resident to be used at his/her discretion. Application deadline is Dec 31. There is a $10 application fee.

Phil Killian Directing Fellowship
Oregon Shakespeare Festival; Box 158; Ashland, OR 97520
(541) 482-2111; 482-0446 FAX
E-mail: timb@orshakes.org
Web: http://www.orshakes.org
Timothy Bond, Associate Artistic Director

The Phil Killian Directing Fellowship is offered through nomination of a national advisory committee to early-career directors interested in large-scale classical theatre and Shakespeare. To qualify for nomination, the director must have directed at least three Equity-level, professional productions. The Fellow functions as an assistant director on 2 large-scale classical productions, and directs a public play reading over a 3 to 4 month period. Housing, travel and a $1,000 per month stipend are provided. (See Chapter 7: Regional Theatre Opportunities.)

Regional Artists Project Grants Program
Arts and Science Council of Charlotte/Mecklenburg; 227 West Trade St, Suite 250; Charlotte, NC 28202
(704) 372-9667; 372-8210 FAX
Anne Porges, Grants Officer

Regional Artists Project Grants Program supports accomplished artists in designated North and South Carolina counties, seeking to advance their professional careers with grants ranging from $500 to $1,500. Students are not eligible. Projects must take place between Oct 1 and Jun 30. Application deadline is Aug 3.

Repertorio Español: Edward and Sally Van Lier Fellowships
Repertorio Español; 138 East 27th St; New York, NY 10016
(212) 889-2850; 686-3732 FAX
Allison Astor-Vargas, Executive Assistant

Early-career directors are given the opportunity to direct the first professional project of their choosing in the Spanish language. The fellowship gives directors a chance to expand artistically, and to learn the business and financial aspects of the profession. Directors must be under 30 years old and New York City residents. Each director is given a modest production budget and is expected to cast their production; oversee all production matters including rehearsals, design and sound; and prepare for the production's opening.

Stage Directors and Choreographers (SDC) Foundation
1501 Broadway, Suite 1701; New York, NY 10036
(212) 302-5359; 302-6195 FAX
E-mail: ddstar@compuserve.com
Web: http://www.arts-online.com/sdnc.htm
David Diamond, Executive Director

The Professional Guest Director/Choreographer Program is a grant program available to members of the Society of Stage Directors and Choreographers (SSDC), which underwrites the hiring of a professional director or choreographer to work on a particular project. The grant amount varies, but is intended to cover half of the director or choreographer's professional fee under a League of Resident Theatre (LORT) contract. The goal of the program is to encourage smaller theatres to invite directors and choreographers with higher profiles to work in the theatres. Application deadline is Feb. (See Chapter 2: Career Development; Chapter 5: Service Organizations.)

Theatre Communications Group (TCG)
355 Lexington Ave; New York, NY 10017-0217
(212) 697-5230; 983-4847 FAX
E-mail: grants@tcg.org
Web: http://www.tcg.org
Emilya Cachapero, Director of Grant Programs

The NEA/TCG Career Development Program for Directors supports outstanding directors seeking careers in America's not-for-profit professional theatre. It offers recipients the opportunity to spend 6 months developing their creative skills and expanding their knowledge of the field by working with one or more senior artists. Placements are hand-tailored, matching the needs and goals of the recipient with appropriate and challenging assignments. Candidates must have directed at least 3 fully staged professional productions, among other requirements. An award of $17,500 will go to 6 directors per grant cycle. Application deadline is Dec 31, 1998. Assignments commence no earlier than Oct 1 and conclude by Sept 30, 2 years later.

The National Theatre Artist Residency Program is designed to foster both new and expanded relationships between theatres and individual artists. It targets accomplished artists (including directors and choreographers) who have created a significant body of work. The grant requires that artists be on-site at participating theatres full-time for a minimum of 4 months during an overall grant period of up to 2 years. While a residency may be oriented toward the development of one or more theatre works, the primary focus of the program is on residencies that create new full-time roles for artists within institutions, as well as programs designed purely for artistic growth and exploration. Awards range from $25,000, $50,000 or $100,000 for the theatre/artist(s) partnerships. Guidelines are available after Sept 15. (See Chapter 5: Service Organizations.)

STATE ARTS COUNCILS AND AGENCIES

Many state arts councils offer grants or have programs for not-for-profit arts organizations and individual artists, which include artists-in-residence; traveling and guest artist programs; programs in the schools, community centers, parks and recreation centers; and much more. Recipients of these awards are typically residents of the grantmaking state. The following list of state arts councils will get you started. We have listed only contact information because most arts councils offer many grants and opportunities (too numerous to list in this publication), and should be contacted directly for in-depth information.

Web Sites are an excellent way of seeing the broad scope of grants provided by state arts councils. A Web Site that has links to all arts councils is Arts Over America's (http://www.nasaa-arts.or/new/nasaa/gateway/gateway.html), which contains a click-on map for easy access to all of the following state arts councils.

Alabama State Council on the Arts
201 Monroe St; Montgomery, AL 36130-1800
(334) 242-4076; 240-3269 FAX
Web: http://www.bham.com/asca/

Alaska State Council on the Arts
411 West 4th Ave, Suite 1E; Anchorage, AK 99501-2343
(907) 269-6610, (888) 278-7424 (toll free); (907) 269-6601 FAX
E-mail: asca@alaska.net
Web: http://www.educ.state.ak.us/ASCA/home/html

American Samoa Council on Culture, Arts and Humanities
Box 1540; Office of the Governor; Pago Pago, AS 96799
(011) 684-633-4347; 684-633-2059 FAX
Web: http://www.nasaa-arts.org/new/nasaa/gateway/AS.html

Arizona Commission on the Arts
417 West Roosevelt St; Phoenix, AZ
(602) 255-5882; 256-0282 FAX
E-mail: artscomm@primenet.com
Web: http:/az.arts.asu.edu/arscomm/

Arkansas Arts Council
1500 Tower Building; 323 Center St; Little Rock, AR 72201
(501) 324-9700; 324-9154 FAX
E-mail: info@dah.state.ar.us
Web: http://www.heritage.state.ar.us/aac/

California Arts Council
1300 I St, Suite 930; Sacramento, CA 95814
(916) 322-6555; 322-6575 FAX
E-mail: cac@cwo.com
Web: http://www.cac.ca.gov/

Colorado Council on the Arts
750 Pennsylvania St; Denver, CO 80203
(303) 894-2617; 894-2615 FAX
E-mail: coloarts@ix.netcom.com

Connecticut Arts Council
755 Main St, Gold Building; Hartford, CT 06103
(860) 566-4770; 566-6462 FAX
Web: http://www.cslnet.ctstateu.edu/cca/

Delaware Division of the Arts
820 North French St; Wilmington, DE 19801-3509
(302) 577-8278; 577-6561 FAX
Web: http://www.artsdel.org

District of Columbia Commission on the Arts and Humanities
415 12th St, NW, Suite 804; Washington, DC 20004
(202) 724-5613; 727-4135 FAX
Web: http://www.capaccess.org/dccah/

Florida Division of Cultural Affairs
Florida Department of State; The Capitol; Tallahassee, FL 32399-0250
(850) 487-2980; 922-5259 FAX
Web: http://www.dos.state.fl.us

Georgia Council for the Arts
260 14th St NW, Suite 401; Atlanta, GA 30318
(404) 685-ARTS; 685-2788 FAX
Web: http://www.ganet.org/

Guam Council on the Arts & Humanities Agency
Office of the Governor; Box 2950; Agana, Guam 96910
(011) 671-475-2242; 671-472-2781 FAX
Web: http://www.nasaa-arts.org/new/nasaa/gateway/Guam.html

State Foundation on Culture and the Arts (Hawaii)
44 Merchant St; Honolulu, HI 96813
(808) 586-0300; 586-0308 FAX
E-mail: sfca@sfca.state.hi.us
Web: http://www.state.hi.us/sfca/

Idaho Commission on the Arts
Box 83720; Boise, ID 83720-0008
(208) 334-2119, (800) 278-3863; (208) 334-3488 FAX
Web: http://www2.state.id.us/arts/

Illinois Arts Council
100 West Randolph, Suite 10-500; Chicago, IL 60601
(312) 814-6750, (800) 237-6994 (toll free in Illinois); (312) 814-1471 FAX
Web: http://www.state.il.us/agency/lacl

Indiana Arts Commission
402 West Washington St, Room 072; Indianapolis, IN 46204-2741
(317) 232-1268; 232-5595 FAX
Web: http://www.ai.org/iac/

Iowa Arts Council
600 East Locust; De Moines, IA 50319-0290
(515) 281-4451; 242-6498 FAX
Web: http://www.state.ia.us/government/ldca/lac/

Kansas Arts Commission
Jayhawk Tower; 700 SW Jackson, Suite 1004; Topeka, KS 66603-3758
(785)-296-3335; 296-4989 FAX
Web: http://www.nasaa-arts.org/new/nasaa/gateway/KS.html

Kentucky Arts Council
31 Fountain Pl; Frankfort, KY 40601
(502) 564-3757; 564-2839 FAX
E-mail: kyarts@arts.smag.state.ky.us
Web: http://www.state.ky.us/agencies/arts/kachome.html

Louisiana Division of the Arts
Box 44247; Baton Rouge, LA 70804-4247
(504) 342-8180; 342-8173 FAX
E-mail: arts@crt.state.la.us
Web: http://www.crt.state.la.us/crt/ocd/doapage/doapage.html

Maine Arts Commission
55 Capitol St; State House Station 25; Augusta, ME 04333-0025
(207) 287-2724; 287-2335 FAX
Web: http://www.mainarts.com/

Maryland State Arts Council
601 North Howard St; Baltimore, MD 21201
(410) 333-8232; 333-1062 FAX
Web: http://www.msac.org/

Massachusetts Cultural Council
120 Boylston St; Boston, MA 02116-4600
(617) 727-3668, (800) 232-0960 (toll free in Massachusetts);
(617) 727-0044 FAX
Web: http://www.nasaa-arts.org/new/nasaa/gateway/MA.html

Michigan Council for Arts and Cultural Affairs
Executive Plaza, 11th Floor; 1200 Sixth Ave;
Detroit, MI 48226-2461
(313) 256-3731; 256-3781 FAX
Web: http://www.cis.state.mi.us/arts/contact.htm

Minnesota State Arts Board
Park Square Court; 400 Sibley St, Suite 200; St. Paul, MN 55102-1949
(612) 215-1600; 215-1602 FAX
Web: http://www.nasaa-arts.org/new/nasaa/gateway/MN.html

Mississippi Arts Commission
239 North Lamar St, 2nd Floor; Jackson, MS 39201
(601) 359-6030; 359-6008 FAX
Web: http://www.arts.state.ms.us/

Missouri Arts Council
111 North 7th St, Suite 105; St. Louis, MO 63101-2188
(314) 340-6845; 340-7215 FAX
Web: http://www.ecodeu.state.mo.us/moarts.council/

Montana Arts Council
City County Building; 316 North Park Ave, Room 252;
Helena, MT 59620-2201
(406) 444-6430; 444-6548 FAX
E-mail: montana@artswire.org
Web: http://www.nasaa-arts.org/new/nasaa/gateway/MT.html

Nebraska Arts Council
Joslyn Castle Carriage House; 3838 Davenport St;
Omaha, NE 68131-2329
(402) 595-2122, (800) 341-4067; (402)595-2334 FAX
Web: http://www.gps.k12.ne.us/nac_web_site/nac.htm

Nevada Sate Council on the Arts
Capitol Complex; 602 North Curry St, Carson City, NV 89710
(702) 687-6680; 687-6688 FAX
Web: http://www.clan.lib.nv.us/dos/ARTS/arts-con.htm

New Hampshire State Council on the Arts
Phenix Hall; 40 North Main St; Concord, NH 03301-4974
(603) 271-2789; 271-3584 FAX
Web: http://www.state.nh.us/nharts/

New Jersey State Council on the Arts
Box 306; Trenton, NJ 08625
(609) 292-6130; 989-1440 FAX
E-mail: barbara@arts.sos.state.nj.us
Web: http://www.artswire.org/Artswire/njsca

New Mexico Arts Division
228 East Palace Ave; Santa Fe, NM 87501
(505) 827-6490; 827-6043 FAX
E-mail: jortiz@oca.state.nm.us.
Web: http://www.nmmnh-abq.mus.nm.us/

New York State Council on the Arts
915 Broadway; New York, NY 10010
(212) 387-7000; 387-7164 FAX
Web: http://www.artswire.org/~nysca/

North Carolina Arts Council
Department of Cultural Resources; Raleigh, NC 27611
(919) 733-2821; 733-4834 FAX
E-mail: mregan@ncacmail.dcr.state.nc.us

North Dakota Council on the Arts
418 East Broadway, Suite 70; Bismarck, ND 58501-4086
(701) 328-3954; 328-3963 FAX
Web: http://pioneer.state.nd.us/arts/

**Commonwealth Council for Arts and Culture
(Northern Mariana Islands)**
Box 5553, CHRB; Saipan, MP 96950
(011) 670-322-9982, 670-322-9983; 670-322-9028 FAX
E-mail: galaidi@gtepacifica.net
Web: http://www.nasaa-arts.org/new/nasaa/gateway/NorthernM.html

Ohio Arts Council
727 East Main St; Columbus, OH 43205-1796
(614) 466-2613; 466-4494 FAX
Web: http://www.oac.ohio.gov/

Oklahoma Arts Council
Box 52001-2001; Oklahoma City, OK 73152-2001
(405) 521-2931; 521-6418 FAX
E-mail: okarts@tmn.com
Web: http://www.oklaosf.state.ok.us/~arts/

Oregon Arts Commission
775 Summer St NE; Salem, OR 97310
(503) 986-0087, (800) 233-3306 (toll free in Oregon); (503) 986-0260 FAX
E-mail: oregon@artswire.org
Web: http://art.econ.state.or.us/

Pennsylvania Council on the Arts
Finance Building, Room 216; Harrisburg, PA 17120
(717) 787-6883; 783-2538 FAX
Web: http://artsnet.heinz.cmu.edu/pca/

Institute of Puerto Rican Culture
Box 9024184; San Juan, PR
(787) 725-5137; 724-8393 FAX
Web: http://www.nasaa-arts.org/news/nasaa/gateway/PR.html

Rhode Island State Council on the Arts
95 Cedar St, Suite 103; Providence RI 02903
(401) 222-3880; 521-1351 FAX
Web: http://www.modcult.brown.edu/RISCA/

South Carolina Arts Commission
1800 Gervais St; Columbia, SC 29201
(803) 734-8696; 734-8526 FAX
Web: http://www.midnet.sc.edu/scac/artweb.htm

South Dakota Arts Council
Office of the Arts; Department of Education & Cultural Affairs;
800 Governors Dr; Pierre, SD 57501-2294
(605) 773-3131, (800) 423-6665 (toll free in South Dakota);
(605)773-6962 FAX
E-mail: sdac@stlib.state.sd.us
Web: http://www.state.sd.us/state/executive/deca/sdarts/sdarts.htm

Tennessee Arts Commission
Citizens Plaza; 401 Charlotte Ave; Nashville, TN 37243-0780;
(615) 741-1701; 741-8559 FAX
Web: http://www.arts.state.tn.us/

Texas Commission on the Arts
Box 13406; Capitol Station; Austin, TX 78711-3406
(512) 463-5535, (800) 252-9415 (toll free message line); (512) 475-2699 FAX
E-mail: frontdesk@arts.state.tx.us
Web: http://www.arts.state.tx.us/

Utah Arts Council
617 East South Temple St; Salt Lake City, UT 84102
(801) 236-7555; 236-7556 FAX
E-mail: bstephen@arts.state.ut.us

Vermont Arts Council on the Arts
136 State St; Drawer 33; Montpelier, Vermont 05633-6001
(802) 828-3291; 828-3363 FAX
E-mail: info@arts.vca.state.vt.us
Web: http://www.state.vt.us/vermont-arts

Virgin Islands Council on the Arts
41-42 Norre Gade, Box 103; St. Thomas, Virgin Islands 00804
(809) 774-5984; 774-6206 FAX
Web: http://www.nasaa-arts.org/new/nasaa/gateway/VI.html

Virginia Commission for the Arts
223 Governor St, 2nd Floor; Richmond, VA 23219-2010
(804) 225-3132; 225-4327 FAX
Web: http://www.artswire.org/~vacomm/

Washington State Arts Commission
Box 42675; Olympia WA 98504-2675
(360) 753-3860; 586-5351 FAX
Web: http://www.wa.gov/art

West Virginia Commission on the Arts
1900 Kanawha Blvd, East; Charleston, WV 25305-0300
(304) 558-0240; 558-2779 FAX
Web: http://www.wvlc.wvnet.edu/culture/arts.html

Wisconsin Arts Board
101 East Wilson St, 1st Floor; Madison, WI 53702
(608) 266-0190; 267-0380 FAX
E-mail: rtertin@arts.state.wi.us
Web: http://www.arts.state.wi.us/

Wyoming Arts Council
2320 Capitol Ave; Cheyenne, WY 82002
(307) 777-7742; 777-5499 FAX
Web: http://commerce.state.wy.us/cr/arts/index.html

REGIONAL ARTS ORGANIZATIONS

Information from the following organizations is also available via Arts Over America (Web: http://www.nasaa-arts.or/new/nasaa/gateway/gateway.html).

Arts Midwest
528 Hennepin Ave, Suite 310; Minneapolis MN 55403-1899
(612) 341-0755; 341-0902 FAX
Web: http://www.artsmidwest.org/state.htm
David J. Fraher, Executive Director

Arts Midwest is a not-for-profit organization, which funds artists and arts organizations. Arts Midwest works in partnership with arts organizations in the Midwest, and state art agencies including the Illinois Arts Council, Indiana Arts Commission, Iowa Arts Council, Michigan Council for Arts and Cultural Affairs, Minnesota State Arts Board, North Dakota Council on the Arts, The Ohio Arts Council, South Dakota Arts Council, and the Wisconsin Arts Board.

Consortium for Pacific Arts & Culture
1580 Makaloa St, Suite 930; Honolulu, HI 96814-3220
(808) 946-7381; 955-2722 FAX
E-mail: cpac@pixi.com
Web: http://www.nasaa-arts.org/new/nasaa/gateway/CPAC.html
Merrie Carol Grain, Director

The Consortium is committed to artistic excellence through the presentation and encouragement of opportunities, growth and exchange of traditional and contemporary arts; by fostering and perpetuating in the arts within the Pacific

region; and through the promotion and cultivation of increased global awareness and appreciation of Pacific cultures.

Mid Atlantic Arts Foundation

22 Light St, Suite 300; Baltimore, MD 21202
(410) 539-6656
Web: http://www.charm.net/-midarts/

The Foundation provides support through grants, technical assistance and
information to artists and arts organizations in Delaware, District of Columbia, Maryland, New Jersey, New York, Pennsylvania, Virginia, the U.S. Virgin Islands and West Virginia.

Mid-America Arts Alliance

912 Baltimore Ave, Suite 700; Kansas City, MO 64105
(816) 421-1388; 421-3918 FAX
Henry Moran, Executive Director

The Alliance offers programs including the Performing Arts Programs, Exhibits-
USA, speakers, workshops, symposium subsidies, international programs and
Mid-America Productions. Other services offered include professional develop-
ment and technical services. The Alliance works in partnership with arts organi-
zations in Arkansas, Kansas, Missouri, Nebraska, Oklahoma and Texas. The
Heartland Arts Fund is a new venture of Arts Midwest and Mid-America Arts
Alliance. The Fund offers performing arts presenters and artists in 15 states
an extensive array of presenting opportunities.

New England Foundation for the Arts (NEFA)

330 Congress St, 6th Floor; Boston, MA 02215
(617) 951-0010; 951-0016 FAX
Web: http://www.nefa.org/

NEFA is a cooperative program with the state arts agencies of Connecticut,
Maine, Massachusetts, New Hampshire, Rhode Island and Vermont.

Southern Arts Federation
181 14th St, NE, Suite 400; Atlanta, GA 30309-7603
(404) 874-7244; 873-2148 FAX
Jeffrey Kesper, Executive Director

A not-for-profit arts organization which creates partnerships, assists in artist development, and presents and promotes southern artwork in partnership with arts organizations in Alabama, Florida, Georgia, Kentucky, North Carolina, South Carolina, Louisiana, Mississippi and Tennessee.

Western States Arts Federation (WESTAF)
1543 Champa St, Suite 220; Denver, CO 80202
(303) 629-1166; 629-9717
E-mail: casey@artswire.org
Web: http://www.westaf.org

WESTAF is dedicated to the creative advancement and preservation of the arts. Focused on serving artists, arts organizations and state arts agencies of the western U.S., WESTAF fulfills its mission by taking an innovative approach to providing support, programs and experience, which strengthen the financial, organizational and policy infrastructure of the arts. The organization focuses on the areas of presenting, literature, visual arts, Native American arts and folk arts. In addition, it is involved in a variety of research and technology development projects, including studies on the economic impact of the arts.

CHAPTER 5

SERVICE ORGANIZATIONS AND UNIONS

This chapter contains a list of organizations that offer services to the theatrical community in the United States. Listed here are professional unions ranging from the Actors' Equity Association (AEA) to the Society of Stage Directors and Choreographers (SSDC); professional leagues ranging from the Drama League to the League of Professional Theatre Women/New York; professional alliances ranging from the Alliance of Resident Theatres/New York to the National Alliance for Musical Theatre; and many more organizations that offer services ranging from presenting the performing arts to developing the community of stage directors in a specific geographical area.

All listings are in alphabetical order and contain contact information and a brief description of services offered. For further information on specific programs, eligibility and dues (which may accompany membership to a service organization) contact the organization directly.

Actors' Equity Association
165 West 46th St; New York, NY 10036
(212) 869-8530; 719-9815 FAX
Web: http://www.actorsequity.org
Ron Silver, President

AEA is the union representing professional actors, singers, dancers and stage managers. For further information regarding union guidelines please contact AEA offices in New York, Chicago, Orlando, Los Angeles or San Francisco directly.

Alliance of Resident Theatres/New York
131 Varick St, Room 904; New York, NY 10013
(212) 989-5257; 989-4880 FAX
E-mail: artnewyork@aol.com
Virginia P. Louloudes, Executive Director

A.R.T./New York serves as an information resource and network for 280 member New York City not-for-profit theatre companies. It provides services to increase managerial strength, and serves as an advocate for the New York City theatre community by promoting solidarity, growth and excellence in New York City's not-for-profit theatres. Programs include the Elizabeth Steinway Chapin Real Estate Loan Fund; a cash-flow loan fund; the Nancy Quinn Fund, which provides technical assistance, workshops and cash awards to small and emerging companies; and the annual "Passport to Off Broadway" campaign, which offers discount tickets to theatregoers. A.R.T./New York also offers liability insurance, payroll and credit-card processing and long-distance telephone services. Publications include a membership directory and the quarterly *Hot Seats*, which lists theatre productions, neighborhood maps and information. (See Chapter 8: Producing Your Own Work.)

Alternate ROOTS
1083 Austin Ave; Atlanta, GA 30307
(404) 577-1079; 577-7991 FAX
Greg Carraway, Managing Director

Alternate ROOTS (Regional Organization of Theatres South) serves as a catalyst for the exchange of work, ideas and information among southern performing artists and arts organizations. Services include newsletters, annual meetings, regional workshops, artistic assistance, touring subsidies, showcases and festivals.

American Alliance for Theatre and Education
c/o Department of Theatre, Arizona State University
Box 872002; Tempe, AZ 85287-2002
(602) 965-6064; 965-5351 FAX
E-mail: aateinfo@asuvm.inre.asu.edu
Web: http://www.aate.com
Gretta Berghammer, President

AATE provides a communications network for theatre artists and K–12 educators who work with and perform for young people. The association coor-
dinates an annual conference and sponsors the Unpublished Play Reading
Project. Publications include *AATE Newsletter, Youth Theatre Journal, STAGE
of the Art*, curriculum standards, advocacy documents and *Education Center-
stage!*, which profiles education/outreach programs of regional and professional theatres for young audiences.

American Arts Alliance
805 15th St NW, Suite 500; Washington, DC 20005
(202) 289-1776; 371-6601 FAX
Jan Denton, Director

The Alliance represents not-for-profit professional performing, exhibiting
and presenting institutions across the country that are affiliated with the American Symphony Orchestra League, Association of Art Museum Directors,
Association of Performing Arts Presenters, Dance/USA, Opera America and
Theatre Communications Group. The Alliance works to advance support for
the arts with Congress and other branches of the federal government, and to
coordinate grassroots advocacy.

American Council for the Arts
1 East 53rd St; New York, NY 10022-4021
(212) 223-ARTS; 223-4415 FAX
E-mail: infor@artsusa.org
Web: http://artsusa.org/
Virginia Rhodus, General Manager

ACA is a multidisciplinary arts service organization which serves as a source
of legislative news; advises arts administrators, educators and elected officials;
publishes periodicals and books; sponsors national and regional symposiums
on arts issues; and provides information services to arts managers, artists and
others through ArtsUSA, their Web Site and by serving as a national information clearinghouse and archive for arts policy research.

American Theatre Critics Association

c/o Theatre Service; Box 15282; Evansville, IN 47716
(812) 474-0549; 474-4168 FAX
E-mail: ts@evansville.edu
Patricia Angotti, Membership Services

ATCA serves its member critics by publishing a newsletter and a periodic compilation of theatre reviews, and by holding two annual meetings. Yearly, it recommends a regional professional theatre to receive a Tony Award, votes new members into the Theatre Hall of Fame and selects a distinguished play produced outside New York for a $1,000 prize and inclusion in the *Best Plays* series, published by Limelight Editions.

Arts, Crafts and Theatre Safety

181 Thompson St, #23; New York, NY 10012-2586
(212) 777-0062
E-mail: 75054.2542@compuserve.com
Web: http://www.caseweb.com/acts/
Monona Rossol, President

A not-for-profit organization which provides health, safety and industrial hygiene services, ACTS publishes a monthly newsletter, answers inquiries, refers clients to doctors and other sources of help, provides educational materials and speakers and aids theatres in complying with occupational safety and health regulations in the U.S. and Canada.

Arts International Program

(See Chapter 9: Working Abroad and Foreign Festivals.)

Asian American Arts Alliance

74 Varick St, Suite 302; New York, NY 10013-1914
(212) 941-9208; 941-7978 FAX
E-mail: artsalliance@earthlink.net
Lillian Cho, Executive Director

Asian American Arts Alliance is dedicated to increasing the support, recognition and appreciation of art created by Asian-American artists in the New York area. Primarily a service and networking organization for individual artists and organization members, the Alliance also sponsors public forums and provides technical assistance and funding for Asian-American artists and organizations. Publications include directories of Asian-American artists and a bimonthly newsletter, which includes a listing of resources and opportunities for Asian-

American artists and a calendar of events, performances and exhibits throughout the country. (See Chapter 8: Producing Your Own Work.)

A.S.K. Theater Projects
11845 West Olympic Blvd, Suite 1250 West; Los Angeles, CA 90064
(310) 478-3200; 478-5300 FAX
E-mail: askplay@primenet.com
Web: http://www.askplay.org
Kym Eisner, Executive Director

A.S.K. Theater Projects, a national resource for the theatre and its artists, facilitates the creation of new work through a broad range of artistic and educational programs. A.S.K. offers a year-round schedule of readings, practical labs, publications, on-line services and workshop productions, and regularly hosts symposia, festivals, caucuses and labs as forums for exploring issues vital to the theatre.

ASSITEJ/USA
Box 22365; Seattle, WA 98122-0365
(206) 392-2147; 443-0442 FAX
E-mail: assitej@aol.com
Web: http://www.exposurel.com/clients/assitej/toc.htm/
Tom Pechar, President

ASSITEJ/USA, the U.S.Center for the 60-nation International Association of Theatre for Children and Young People, is a national membership organization which promotes the development of professional theatre for young audiences and families in the U.S., and the international interchange of information and artists. It publishes a quarterly bulletin and biannual journal, operates an international playscript exchange and sponsors international seminars, festivals and conferences.

The Association for Theatre in Higher Education
Box 9098; Berkeley, CA 94709-0098
(800) ATHE-737
E-mail: jdolan@email.gc.cuny.edu
Jill Dolan, President

ATHE represents professors of university and college theatres and post-secondary professional training programs throughout the U.S. Programs include national conferences, publications, awards, advocacy and support services. Membership is open to individuals and organizations.

Association of Hispanic Arts
250 West 26th St, 4th Floor; New York, NY 10001
(212) 727-7227; 727-0549 FAX
Sandra M. Perez, Executive Director

AHA is a multidisciplinary organization which supports Hispanic arts organizations and individual artists with technical assistance, planning, financial management systems, identifications of new and emerging Hispanic playwrights and marketing efforts geared toward increasing audiences. Publications include *AHA!*, *Hispanic Arts News* and a monthly newsletter. (See Chapter 8: Producing Your Own Work.)

Association of Independent Video and Filmmakers
304 Hudson St, 6th Floor; New York, NY 10013
(212) 807-1400; 463-8519 FAX
E-mail: info@aivf.org
Web: http://www.aivf.org
Ruby Lerner, Executive Director

The Association is a national trade organization of 5000 independent film and video makers. This organization can help directors and choreographers wishing to explore these media. They publish *Independent Film and Video Monthly* magazine, as well as books related to the field.

Association of Performing Arts Presenters
1112 16th St NW, Suite 400; Washington, DC 20036
(202) 833-2787; 833-1543 FAX
E-mail: artspres@artspresenters.org
Web: http://www.artspresenters.org
Susan Farr, Executive Director

The Association provides services to organizations involved in presenting the performing arts. It administers grantmaking programs, publishes a bimonthly magazine and conducts a variety of advocacy and continuing education activities. It provides a performing arts database, research projects, workshops, seminars, books and a regranting program: the Lila Wallace Reader's Digest Arts Partners Program. APAP's annual conference in New York City brings together presenters, managers, artists and other professionals each December to exchange resources, see work and meet colleagues.

Association of Theatrical Press Agents and Managers
165 West 46th St; New York, NY 10036
(212) 719-3666; 302-1585 FAX
Maria A. Somma, President

ATPAM is the union representing theatrical press agents, publicity and marketing specialists, company managers and house and facilities managers. ATPAM represents individuals working on Broadway, Off-Broadway, on the road, at the opera, the symphony, in dance, cabarets and in not-for-profit and regional theatres across America and Canada.

Atlanta Coalition of Theatres
173 14th St, Suite 304; Atlanta, GA 30309
(404) 873-1185; 733-4756 FAX
E-mail: atlantatheatres@mindspring.com
Web: http://www.atlantatheatres.org
Kim Patrick Bitz, Executive Director

ACT, a partnership of metro-Atlanta's 60-plus theatre and dance companies, is dedicated to facilitating collaborative programs, services and initiatives, which provide a nurturing environment for the performing arts.

Black Theatre Network
2603 Northwest 13th St, Suite 312; Gainesville, FL 32609
(352) 495-2116; 495-2051 FAX
E-mail: manicho@aol.com
Mikell Pinkney, President

BTN is a national network of professional artists, scholars and community groups founded to provide a national forum for discussion of black theatre; to collect and disseminate information; and to encourage black dramatists and production of plays about the black experience. Members attend conferences and receive complimentary copies of BTN publications.

Chicago Directors' Forum
c/o Effective Theatre
Box 18423; Chicago, IL 60618
(773) 918-8871
E-mail: DirForum@aol.com
Web: http://www.japerformance.com/cdf
Elizabeth Lucas, Chair

The Chicago Directors' Forum's mission is to develop a resource organization for Chicago-area directors. CDF strives to develop a community of stage directors, and provide networking opportunities between stage directors and the general artistic community. CDF seeks to facilitate the exchange of ideas and stimulate artistic growth through regular meetings and discussions, Directors' Nights Out, workshops and mentoring programs. CDF produces a bimonthly newsletter/postcard that informs members of upcoming events.

Collaborative Arts Project (CAP) 21
18 West 18th St, 6th Floor; New York, NY 10011
(212) 807-0202; 807-0166 FAX
Frank Ventura, Artistic Director
Peter T. Van Wyck, Managing Director

CAP21 is a not-for-profit theatre development company and conservatory which dedicates itself to the creation of new work, the development of new talent and the building of new audiences. CAP21 cosponsors a Staged-Reading/Work-in-Progress series with the SDCF which allows directors and playwrights the opportunity to present works at various stages in their development in front of an audience. Readings are held every Monday evening at CAP and are free of charge.

Directors Guild of America
7920 Sunset Blvd; Los Angeles, CA 90046
(310) 289-2000; 289-2029 FAX
and
400 North Michigan Ave, Suite 307; Chicago IL 60611
(312) 644-5050; 644-5776 FAX
and
110 West 57th St; New York, NY 10019
(212) 581-0370; 581-1441 FAX
and
330 North Federal Highway; Hollywood FL 33020
(954) 927-3338; 923-8737 FAX
Web: http://www.dga.org

The Directors Guild of America represents more than 10,000 members working in the U.S. and abroad in theatre; industrial, educational and documentary films; television; radio; video; and commercials.

The Drama League
165 West 46th St, Suite 601; New York, NY 10036
(212) 302-2100; 302-2254 FAX
E-mail: dlny@echonyc.com
Web: http://www.echonyc.com/~dlny
Julia Hansen, President

The League develops and nurtures artists and audiences for the theatre. Its national Directors Project provides training, assistant directorships and Equity production opportunities for entry-level and early-career directors; its Seminars for Working Directors program provides a forum for discussion of practical and artistic issues; and the Developing Artist Series and New Directors/New Works programs support new theatrical voices through public presentations of developing work. The League offers lectures, seminars, workshops, theatre ticket services and a monthly newsletter. (See Chapter 2: Career Development.)

The Dramatists Guild
1501 Broadway, Suite 701; New York, NY 10036
(212) 398-9366; 944-0420 FAX
Christopher Wilson, Acting Executive Director

The Guild is a professional association of playwrights, composers and lyricists which works to protect the rights of authors, promote their professional interests and improve the conditions under which they work. All theatre writers are eligible for membership. The Guild counsels members on contracts, copyright issues and other matters; sponsors symposia on professional theatre; and publishes *The Dramatist Guild Quarterly*, the monthly *Dramatists Guild Newsletter* and the *Annual Resource Directory*.

The Field

161 Sixth Ave; New York, NY 10013
(212) 691-6969; 255-2053 FAX
E-mail: thefield@aol.com
Katherine Longstreth, Executive Director

The Field is a not-for-profit organization dedicated to helping independent performing artists develop artistically and professionally through a variety of performance opportunities, workshops, services and publications. Field programs are offered in Atlanta, Chicago, Dallas, Houston, Miami, New York, Philadelphia, San Francisco, Seattle, Toronto and Washington, DC.

Harvestworks: Digital Media Arts

596 Broadway, Suite 602; New York, NY 10012
(212) 431-1130; 431-8473 FAX
E-mail: harvestw@dti.com
Web: http://www.harvestworks.org
Seth Thompson, Business Manager

Harvestworks is a not-for-profit arts organization which provides support services to artists who use sound, pictures and technology as a creative medium. Their mission is to foster the creation of works by artists seeking to expand the vocabulary of digital art, and to increase the audience for that work. In addition to a recording studio and multimedia lab, Harvestworks hosts an Artist-in-Residence program; a Composer Contact Service; classes; Listin In: a series of presentations by artists who use technology; and Tellus: an audio series on cassette and compact disc. Harvestworks invites composers, film and video makers, choreographers and installation artists to use their recording and multimedia production studios.

Hatch-Billops Collection
491 Broadway, 7th Floor; New York, NY 10012-4412
(212) 966-3231; 966-3231 FAX (call first)
E-mail: hatchbillops@worldnet.att.net
James V. Hatch, Executive Secretary

The Hatch-Billops Collection is a not-for-profit research library specializing in black American art and theatre history. It was founded in 1975 to collect and preserve primary and secondary resource materials in the black cultural arts, and to make them available to artists, scholars and the general public; and to develop programs in the arts which use the collection's resources. It is an excellent resource for information, photographs, posters, clippings, letters, brochures, periodicals, books and over 1800 oral-history tapes. The collection is available by appointment only.

HOLA: Hispanic Organization of Latin Actors
250 West 65th St; New York, NY 10023-6403
(212) 595-8286; 799-6718 FAX
E-mail: holagram@aol.com
Manuel Alfaro, Executive Director

HOLA serves as a liaison between Hispanic talent and the entertainment industry through its talent referral services, a directory, showcases of Hispanic work and touring programs.

Institute of Outdoor Drama
University of North Carolina
CB3240 Nations Bank Plaza, Suite 201; Chapel Hill, NC 27599-3240
(919) 962-1328; 962-4212 FAX
E-mail: outdoor@unc.edu
Web: http://www.unc.edu.depts/outdoor/
Scott J. Parker, Director

A public service agency of the University of North Carolina at Chapel Hill, the Institute serves as the national clearinghouse for more than 95 outdoor theatres, and as a resource for organizations and individuals concerned with the production of outdoor historical drama. It conducts feasibility studies for proposed outdoor drama projects, sponsors a national conference and national auditions and publishes a quarterly newsletter, the *Directory of Outdoor Historical Drama in America.*

International Theatre Institute of the United States (ITI/US)
47 Great Jones St; New York, NY 10012
(212) 254-4141; 254-6814 FAX
E-mail: info@iti-usa.org
Web: http://www.iti-usa.org
Martha W. Coigney, Director

ITI/US was founded to promote the exchange of knowledge and practice in the theatre arts. The Institute operates centers in 96 countries, assists foreign theatre visitors in the U.S. and American theatre representatives traveling abroad, operates an international consultation and information service and maintains a library with material on contemporary theatre in 146 countries. (See Chapter 9: Working Abroad and Foreign Festivals.)

Latin American Theater Artists
30 Grant Ave; San Francisco, CA 94108
(415) 439-2425; 834-3360 FAX
Luis Oropeza, Artistic Director

Latin American Theater Artists is a performing and support organization. LATA produces one full production annually, a reading series of both new and traditional Latin American plays and a children's show. The organization offers a casting and referral service to its dues-paying members, training workshops and a newsletter. LATA primarily serves Bay Area Latinos and Latinas, but is open for membership nationally. Annual dues are $25.

League of Professional Theatre Women/New York
c/o Shari Upbin
300 East 56th St, #2A; New York, NY 10022
(212) 583-0177; 583-0549 FAX
Shari Upbin, President

The League promotes women in all areas of professional theatre, with industry-related opportunities for women, and highlights contributions of theatre women, past and present. Programs include salons, seminars, educational programs, social events, awards and festivals. Annual dues are $75.

Literary Managers and Dramaturgs of the Americas
Box 355 CASTA; City University of New York; Graduate Center;
33 West 42nd St; New York, NY 10036
(212) 642-2657; 642-1977 FAX
E-mail: hbc3@columbia.edu
President

LMDA, a national membership organization, serves more than 300 literary managers, dramaturgs, artistic associates and other theatre professionals through national conferences, regional meetings, an 800-number job phone, a new dramaturg program, a script exchange, a universities program, guides to training programs and internships, production diaries and a newsletter.

Movement Theatre International
Box 29165; Philadelphia, PA 19127-0165
(215) 487-7637; 487-7647 FAX
E-mail: mapedretti@aol.com
Michael A. Pedretti, President/Artistic Director

Serving as a center for the movement arts in the U.S., MTI presents an array of international performers; promotes movement arts to the public; acts as a network for performers, presenters, agents, funders, producers, critics and the press; presents festivals and conferences; sponsors study opportunities with master teachers; and creates opportunities to use movement artists in civic and political environments. MTI also operates a 350-seat theatre in which dance and theatre companies self-produce.

National Alliance for Musical Theatre
330 West 45th St, Lobby B; New York, NY 10036-3854
(212) 265-5376; 582-8730 FAX
E-mail: NAMTheatre@aol.com
Web: http://www.bway.net/namt
Helen Sneed, Executive Director

The Alliance, an association of 85 theatre and opera companies, exists to assist its members in preserving and extending the American musical theatre. Programs include annual conferences; a festival of new musicals; a commissioning fund for members; a new work development arm; shared productions and physical resources; advocacy; research, management and information services; and publications including a newsletter, a set and costume rental registry, a profile directory of member companies and a catalog of new, member-produced musicals available for production.

The National Association of Artists' Organizations (NAAO)
918 F St NW, Suite 611; Washington, DC 20004
(202)347-6350; 347-7376 FAX
E-mail: naao@tmn.com

The National Association of Artists' Organizations is a not-for-profit organization dedicated to serving and promoting artist-run organizations: the primary makers, presenters and supporters of new and emerging work in the visual, performing, literary and interdisciplinary arts.

National Endowment for the Arts
1100 Pennsylvania Ave NW; Washington, DC 20506-0001
(202) 682-5510; 682-5669 FAX
E-mail: boltg@endow.gov
Web: http://www.arts.ednow.gov
Gigi Bolt, Director, Theater and Musical Theater

The NEA is an independent federal agency created to promote and support the arts in the U.S. Funding opportunities for organizations are available according to four themes: Heritage and Preservation, Education and Access, Creation and Presentation, Planning and Stabilization. Support is also available to individual directors, designers and playwrights through programs administered by the Endowment.

National Theatre Workshop of the Handicapped
354 Broome St, Loft 5F; New York, NY 10013
(212) 941-9511; 941-9486 FAX
Rick Curry, Founder and Artistic Director

NTWH is a training, production and advocacy organization serving physically disabled adults who are talented in the performing arts. It is one of the very few places in the country where new dramatic literature on themes of disability is regularly tested and produced. In addition to offering professional instruction in acting, music, voice, movement and playwriting, NTWH maintains a professional repertory theatre company which showcases the talents of its students.

New England Theatre Conference
Department of Theatre, Northeastern University
360 Huntington Ave; Boston, MA 02115
(617) 424-9275; 424-1057 FAX
E-mail: netc@world.com
Corey Boniface, Manager of Operations

The New England Theatre Conference (NETC) is a membership organization primarily, but not exclusively, for New England theatre people, including directors, playwrights, teachers, students and theatre professionals. Services include an annual conference, publication of a member directory and
annual summer theatre auditions. The organization publishes *New England
Theatre Journal* and *NETC News*. Membership dues are $80 for groups, $30
for individuals and $20 for students.

New Jersey Theatre Group
17 Cook Ave; Madison, NJ 07940
(973) 593-0189; 377-4842 FAX
E-mail: njtg@nj.com
Web: http://www.njtheatregroup.org
Laura Aden, Executive Director

Comprised of the 18 not-for-profit Equity theatres across the state, NJTG
encourages collaboration among its members and advocates private and public support of New Jersey theatre. Programs include collective advertising, a
calendar of events, a theatre sampler subscription, management roundtables,
an annual conference, a job bank and annual job fair, Equity and non-Equity
auditions, an arts education outreach handbook, audio-described performances, a free post-show symposium series, a consulting program for developing theatres and an annual awards dinner honoring corporate and foundation benefactors.

New York Public Library for the Performing Arts
521 West 43rd St; New York, NY 10036
(212) 870-1643; 496-5196 FAX
E-mail: rmarx@nypl.org
Web: http://www.nypl.org/research/lpa/lpa.html
Robert Marx, Executive Director
and
Theatre Collection Reference Information
(212) 870-1639; 787-3852 FAX
E-mail: rtaylor@nyppl.org
Bob Taylor, Curator, Billy Rose Theatre Collection
and
Theatre on Film and Tape Archive
(212) 870-1641; 870-1769 FAX
E-mail: bcorwin@nypl.org
Betty L. Corwin, Project Director

The Theatre Collection documents all aspects of popular entertainment—
theatre, film television, radio, circus—through personal papers, scripts,
promptbooks, photographs, reviews, scrapbooks, periodicals and books. Open
to qualified researchers, the Theatre on Film and Tape Archive contains the
world's largest collection of theatrical productions taped during performance,
including Broadway, Off-Broadway, regional theatre performances and informal oral/video histories. (See Chapter 8: Producing Your Own Work.)

Non-Traditional Casting Project
1560 Broadway, Suite 1600; New York, NY 10036
(212) 730-4750; 730-4820 FAX
E-mail: info@ntcp.org
Web: http://www.ntcp.org
Sharon Jensen, Executive Director

The NTCP works to eliminate discrimination and increase participation of
ethnic, female and disabled artists in theatre, film and television. Through its
national talent bank, newsletter, conferences, services and special projects,
NTCP provides the profession with practical means to achieve a culturally
diverse, inclusive theatre. NTCP involves all theatre artists: actors, directors,
playwrights, designers, choreographers, stage managers and administrators.

OPERA America
1156 15th St NW, Suite 810; Washington, DC 20005-3287
(202) 293-4466; 393-0735 FAX
E-mail: frontdesk@operaam.org
Jamie Driver and Diana Hossack, Co-Managers, The Next Stage

OPERA America is the not-for-profit service organization for the professional opera field in North America and allied international members. OPERA America provides a variety of informational, technical and financial services to its membership, and serves as a resource to the media, funders, government agencies and the general public.

Performing Arts Resources/Technical Assistance Project
270 Lafayette St, Suite 810A; New York, NY 10012
Donna Brady, Executive Director

Performing Arts Resources maintains a database of technical personnel, including stage managers, designers, stagehands. PAR/TAP also operates a Set Recycling Hotline that allows theatres to donate sets they are finished with to other companies.

Plaza de la Raza
3540 North Mission Rd; Los Angeles, CA 90031
(213) 223-2475; 223-1804 FAX
E-mail: admin@plazaraza.org
Web: http://www.plazaraza.org
Rose Cano, Executive Director

Founded in 1970, Plaza de la Raza is a cultural center for the arts and education, primarily serving the surrounding community of East Los Angeles. Every 4 years, the Nuevo L.A. Chicago TheatreWorks project develops new one-acts written by Chicano playwrights through 2-week workshops with directors and playwrights.

Society of Stage Directors and Choreographers (SSDC)
1501 Broadway, Suite 1701; New York, NY 10036
(212) 391-1070; 302-6195 FAX
E-mail: ssdc@msn.com
Web: http://www.ssdc.org
Barbara B. Hauptman, Executive Director

The Society of Stage Directors and Choreographers (SSDC) is an independent labor union for stage directors and choreographers. Representatives of the organization collectively bargain contracts with producing organizations, thus creating the national standards for professional stage direction and choreography. The organization has offices in New York City and Los Angeles, which service approximately 1,150 members in the U.S. and abroad. An executive board, elected from the membership, oversees negotiations, sets policy and hires the administrative staff. SSDC publishes a newsletter six times per year, and holds membership meetings twice a year.

The organization was founded in 1959, and the first collectively bargained agreement (for Broadway) was signed in 1962. Today SSDC has collectively bargained agreements covering the jurisdictions of Broadway, Off-Broadway, the League of Resident Theatres (LORT), the Council of Stock Theatres (COST), the Council of Resident Stock Theatres (CORST), the American Dinner Theatre Institute (ATDI), the Association of Non-Profit Theatres (ANTC), Outdoor Musical Stock (OMS) and a non-equity touring contract (TROIKA).

In the interest of insuring a member's property rights and other basic contract protections, SSDC's work rules state that members must work under contract whenever or wherever hired as a stage director and/or choreographer. The union has promulgated contracts for members who wish to work for producers who are not signatories to one of the above collectively bargained agreements. These contracts encompass stage direction and choreography, but also media choreography (commercial, industrial, music videos, etc.). Since these contracts are not collectively bargained, there are no minimum fees. However, tiered health and pension payments which correspond to the fees are established and are not negotiable.

A member's health and pension benefits are under the auspices of the Society-League Health Fund and the Society-League Pension Fund, respectively. A member is eligible to participate in the health plan if they are employed under an SSDC contract and sufficient employer contributions are made to the Society-League Health Fund on their behalf. A member is eligible for a pension once they reach age sixty-five, provided they are "vested," or have worked under SSDC contracts subject to employer pension contributions in each of seven years with no substantial break in service (five-year vesting will be in effect after 9/1/99 for those with SSDC contract employment after that date).

To qualify for SSDC membership, a director and/or choreographer will need to provide proof of professional credits, which the union defines as either paying jobs or jobs on productions with any union affiliations. Members pay an initiation fee and yearly dues, plus an assessment on all fees and royalties earned under contract. Associate Membership is available to early-career directors, college and university professionals, and community theatre directors and choreographers. Associates receive the newsletter, and can call the administrative offices for contract advice, boiler-plate contract text and standard minimums. The main difference between members and associates is that associates are not filing contracts, which is an important distinction as it excludes associates from qualifying for pension and health benefits. The initiation fee and yearly dues for associates are less than that of full members, and an associate's initiation is creditable toward their full member initiation should they wish to upgrade.

S.T.A.G.E. (Society for Theatrical Artists' Guidance and Enhancement)
Box 214820; Dallas, TX 75221
(214) 630-7722; 630-4468 FAX
Mark E. Hawkins, Executive Director

S.T.A.G.E. acts as an information clearinghouse for theatre artists and theatre organizations in the north Texas region. The society maintains a library of plays, theatre texts and resource information; offers counseling on agents, unions, personal marketing and other career-related matters; posts listing of various job opportunities; maintains an audition callboard for regional opportunities in theatre and film; sponsors an actors' showcase and annual general auditions; and produces the longest running new play festival in Dallas.

Stage Directors and Choreographers (SDC) Foundation
1501 Broadway, Suite 1701; New York, NY 10036
(212) 302-5359; 302-6195 FAX
E-mail: ddstar@compuserve.com
E-mail: stagedcf@aol.com
Web: http://www.ssdc.org/foundation
David Diamond, Executive Director

The SDC Foundation offers services dedicated to fostering, promoting and developing the craft and creativity of theatre directors and choreographers nationally. It provides information, training and exposure that will encourage and educate the emerging artist, support and motivate the mid-career artist and sustain and refresh the established artist. Programs offered by the Foundation include Observerships; the Sir John Gielgud Fellowship: places emerging artists with established artists on productions ranging from regional theatre to Broadway; the Lost Treasures of Dance: master classes in theatrical and social dance forms considered "endangered" by dance historians; publications such as the biannual *Journal for Stage Directors and Choreographers* and the Foundation newsletter; the Loewe Fellowships for working artists in the public schools; roundtables and seminars; One-on-One Conversations with directors and choreographers; a Staged Readings/Works-in-Progress series; the Professional Guest Director/Choreographer Program: an incentive grant program, which assists small professional theatres in hiring a director or choreographer whom they might not otherwise afford; and a variety of networking opportunities. Programs are available in New York, Los Angeles, San Francisco, Seattle, Chicago and other cities. (See Chapter 2: Career Development; Chapter 4: Grants, Fellowships.)

Support Center for Non Profit Management
305 7th Ave; New York, NY 10001
(212) 924-6744; 924-9544 FAX
Don Crocker, Executive Director

The Support Center strengthens the leadership and management capacity of not-for-profit and public service organizations to fulfill their mission and vitalize their communities, by providing management training and consulting, disseminating information and resources, and building strategic alliances. Serves the New York/New Jersey area.

Theatre Communications Group
355 Lexington Ave; New York, NY 10017
(212) 697-5230; 983-4847 FAX
Ben Cameron, Executive Director

TCG offers services in three categories: (1) Programs & Services, which incorporates artistic management and government departments, such as the National Theatre Artist Residency Program; NEA/TCG Theatre Residency Program for playwrights, directors and designers; Extended Collaboration Grants; observerships; awards; Absolut Stages (grants to afford artists of color the opportunity to collaborate with not-for-profit theatres in development of new work). (2) TCG Publications, which includes *ArtSEARCH* (a bimonthly listing of theatre- and dance-related jobs); *American Theatre* magazine; TCG Books. (3) Finance & Management, which services membership; development; customer service; internal operations. (See Chapter 4: Grants, Fellowships; Chapter 8: Producing Your Own Work.)

Theatre Puget Sound (TPS)
Box 19643; Seattle, WA 98109
(206) 901-2851
E-mail: spelvin@spelvin.com
Web: http://www.spelvin.com
Cindy Park, Director

TPS is a trade and service organization, which was founded to promote the spiritual and economic necessity of theatre to the public, and to unify and strengthen the theatre community through programs, resources and services. TPS is a member-driven organization whose main goals are the nurturing of a healthy and vibrant theatre community, developing strong ties among the region's theatre professionals, raising the visibility of the region's theatre scene on national and international levels, and finding ways to develop new and diverse audiences. Member benefits include activity discounts and advanced notification to conferences and TPS-produced functions, access to personal income tax assistance through the VITA program, access to health and dental care through the Professional Artists of Seattle (PAST) plan, *Platform* magazine and a monthly newsletter and use of a TPS member E-mail information exchange. Individual yearly membership is $15. Organization membership is based on a sliding scale, and ranges from $35 to $200.

United Scenic Artists, L.U. 829
16 West 61st St; New York, NY 10023
(212) 581-0300; 977-2011 FAX
E-mail: usa829@aol.com/
Web: http://www.frontpage1.shadow.net/usa829fl
Paul Moore, Business Representative

USA is the union which represents scenic designers, art directors, costume designers, lighting designers, stylists, scenic artists and associated craftpersons working in theatre, film and television. USA has offices in New York, Chicago, Los Angeles and Miami.

United States Information Agency
(See Chapter 9: Working Abroad and Foreign Festivals.)

United States Institute for Theatre Technology
6443 Ridings Rd; Syracuse, NY 13206
(315) 463-6463, (800) 93-USITT; (315) 463-6525 FAX
E-mail: usittno@pppmail.appliedtheory.com
Web: http://www.culturenet.ca/usitt
Leon I. Brauner, President

USITT, the American Association for Design and Production Professionals in the Performing Arts, promotes the advancement of knowledge and skills of its members, and facilitates communication among individuals and organizations engaged in all aspects of design and production in the performing arts.

University/Resident Theatre Association
1560 Broadway, Suite 414; New York, NY 10036
(212) 221-1130; 869-2752 FAX
E-mail: urta@aol.com
Web: http://www.urta.com
Scott L. Steele, Executive Director

U/RTA's national membership is comprised of more than 42 theatre training programs and associated resident theatre companies. It serves as a liaison between graduate educational/training institutions and professional theatres. The Contract Management Program offers a contracting employment and consulting system to universities, professional and community theatres, and other organizations unable to engage professional artists (including directors, actors and designers) directly, due to institutional or government restrictions.

Volunteer Lawyers for the Arts
(See Chapter 8: Producing Your Own Work.)

The Z Space Studio
1360 Mission St, #300; San Francisco, CA 94103
(415) 543-9505
E-mail: zspace@avelino.com
Web: http://www.zspace.org
David Dower, Artistic Director

The Z Space Studio is dedicated to developing Bay Area theatre, by providing a wide range of programs aimed at developing new works, developing individual artistic vision, developing the Bay Area audience and creating a bridge from the Bay Area theatre to the nation. Directors and choreographers may participate in their Residency Program, Word for Word, Zeta Readings, Z Commissions, and Z Presents.

CHAPTER 6

AGENTS ATTORNEYS AND PERSONAL MANAGERS

The role of the agent, attorney and personal manager varies greatly depending on the representative-to-client relationship. Each representative listed in this chapter defines his/her role differently, ranging from negotiating contracts to developing a career. Some agents will take on young directors with a professional recommendation or after observation of the artist's work.

Agents typically help a client develop and maintain his/her career, and negotiate contracts directly. An attorney negotiates contracts, and may also give advice on projects based on the client's needs and legal rights. Personal managers typically have fewer clients to whom they offer more personalized care. They will work with a director or choreographer during two key times in his/her career: in the beginning or developmental phase; and after the client's career is established. Personal managers do not negotiate deals directly.

In this chapter you will find a list of many agents, attorneys and personal managers. Listings are in alphabetical order (by name of agency), and contain contact information, and a list of representatives who handle directors, choreographers or both.

Peter Hagan, agent with the Gersh Agency in New York City, describes the role of the agent and his process in taking on a new client.

AGENTS

Agency for the Performing Arts
9200 Sunset Blvd, Suite 900; Los Angeles, CA 90069
(310) 273-0744; 888-4242 FAX
Lee Dinstman, Ana Marie Allessi
Represents: Directors with established TV and film careers

Agents for the Arts
203 West 23rd St; New York, NY 10011
(212) 229-2562; 463-9313 FAX
Carole Russo
Represents: Directors and Choreographers

The Artists Agency
230 West 55th St, #29D; New York, NY 10019
(212) 245-6960; 333-7420 FAX
Jonathan Russo
Represents: Directors

The Barbara Hogenson Agency
165 West End Ave, Suite 19C; New York, NY 10023
(212) 874-8084; 362-3011 FAX
Barbara Hogenson
Represents: Directors and Choreographers

Berman, Boals & Flynn
208 West 30th St, Suite 401; New York, NY 10001
(212) 966-0339; 966-0389 FAX
Lois Berman, Judy Boals, Jim Flynn
Represents: Directors

The Bethel Agency
360 West 53rd St, Suite BA; New York, NY 10019
(212) 664-0455; 664-0462 FAX
Lewis Chambers
Represents: Directors and Choreographers

Beverly Anderson Agency
1501 Broadway, Suite 2008; New York, NY 10036
(212) 944-7773; 944-1034 FAX
Beverly Anderson
Represents: Directors and Choreographers

Bret Adams, Ltd.
448 West 44th St; New York, NY 10036
(212) 765-5630; 265-2212 FAX
Bret Adams, Bruce Ostler, Margi Roundtree
Represents: Directors and Choreographers

Charles Kopelman
22 West 77th St, Suite 51; New York, NY 10024
(212) 874-4557; 579-0687 FAX
Charles Kopelman
Represents: Directors and Choreographers

Don Buchwald & Associates, Inc.
10 East 44th St; New York, NY 10017
(212) 867-1200; 972-3209 FAX
Don Buchwald, Susan Calogerakis, Steven Feinberg, Joanne Nici,
Ricki Olshan, Rachel Sheedy, David Williams
Represents: Directors

Douglas, Gorman, Rothacker & Wilhelm
1501 Broadway, Suite 703; New York, NY 10036
(212) 382-2000; 719-2878 FAX
Jim Wilhelm, Flo Rathacker, Andrew Lawler, Elizabeth Schacter,
Michelle Gerard
Represents: Directors and Choreographers

Duva-Flack Associates
200 West 57th St, Suite 1008; New York, NY 10019
(212) 957-9600; 957-9606 FAX
Bob Duva, Elin Flack, Richard Fisher
Represents: Directors and Choreographers

THE ADVOCATE
PETER HAGAN, AGENT
GERSH AGENCY, NEW YORK CITY

It is difficult to pinpoint when you need representation by an agent. Usually it's when you don't feel equipped to negotiate a contract, you are at a place in your career when you need to move to a higher level or you've received some attention from the press, theatrical community or the public that you want to guide in the right direction.

You may think that if you have an agent your career will shift into another gear. In some circumstances that may be true. However, that's not always the case. It's a combination of many things, one of which can be an agent. At a certain point you definitely need an agent. Whether you are working in the commercial or not-for-profit theatre, you will need an agent to help keep your career on track, and to steer you through increasingly difficult contracts.

If you have never been represented by an agent, and would like to be, the best way to get representation is through a recommendation from someone that you know, and whom the agent respects. Most agents are too busy to go and see a director's work without a referral. We're at the theatre every night, covering shows that our clients have worked on. With the exception of younger agents, who are building a list, it's rare for an agent to take a client on with no referral at all.

How an agent works with you depends on your personality. Some directors want to talk about the basics only, some want to discuss every aspect of the deal, some use the agent as a sounding-board, and rely on the agent's advice and opinions. What works best for me is being part of the director's planning process. I have to know your personality and what your needs are in order to make the right kind of deal for you.

Generally before I get to the point of negotiating a deal there's a period of time during which I work with you and get to know you. Sometimes I'm thrown into a working relationship trial-by-fire, and I have to get to know you very quickly. More often it's over the course of weeks and months that I get to know you and figure out the best way to work with you. It's important to have a working relationship with someone who respects my opinion and intelligence, and whose opinion and intelligence I respect in return. Certainly

continued on next page

THE ADVOCATE CONTINUED

an agent has to admire and be enthusiastic about the creative capabilities of a particular director.

The thing that makes an agent the craziest is when his client second-guesses him. There is a place for informed skepticism, but when it becomes constant it's destructive to the relationship. The fact of the matter is, the agent has been hired by the director to perform a service.

There may be agents who don't do their job, and like any business relationship, one has to be cognizant of the fact that one or the other elements in a relationship may not be successful. The fact is, most of us who are in the theatre do it because we love it. My colleagues are devoted and intelligent, and they know what they're talking about. The ideal relationship between a director and agent is simple: mutual respect and hard work—on both sides.

I give this advice to everyone I work with: the theatre, more than any other art form, is a communal operation. You can't do it by yourself—and I don't mean just putting on a play. You can't survive in the theatre without having an active network of people within the theatre community to rely on, to be your colleagues, your friends, your contacts. You have to build that. If you don't, you're going to find yourself in an isolated position—that will never get you an agent, or by extension, any more of a career than what you've got now. You must work hard to keep from alienating people. You must work hard to keep your contacts alive. When the time comes when you need an agent, you should be able to talk to a friend or a colleague, and get a referral for one, two or five agents. Getting to that point is a process that can take many years.

There is no school for agents, so you'll find that most agents in the theatre started out doing something else, such as acting, writing or producing. Some have worked as attorneys. Many of us have been in the theatre, and in love with the theatre for most of our lives. We have that thing that everybody in the theatre has—an enormous sense of accomplishment upon seeing a theatre piece "complete" and on the stage.

Agents aren't lawyers, psychotherapists, critics, bookkeeper/accountants or mentors. We are a combination of all of those things to varying degrees, at any given moment during the day, and at any given moment in a client's career. An agent's job can be aggravating and stressful at times—an agent is usually trying to get a producer to give his client something he doesn't want to give. But, that's what the agent is there for—to be the client's advocate.

Epstein Wyckoff & Associates
311 West 43rd St; New York, NY 10036
(212) 586-9110; 586-8019 FAX
Gary Epstein, Mark Feischman
Represents: Directors and Choreographers

Fifi Oscard Associates
24 West 40th St; New York, NY 10018
(212) 764-1100; 840-5019 FAX
Francis Del Duca
Represents: Directors and Choreographers

Flora Roberts, Inc.
157 West 57th St; New York, NY 10019
(212) 355-4165; 246-7138 FAX
Flora Roberts, Sarah Douglas
Represents: Directors and Choreographers

Gersh Agency
232 North Canon Dr; Beverly Hills, CA 90210
(310) 274-6611; 274-4035 FAX
David Gersh, Michael Arlook, Maryann Kelly
and
130 West 42nd St, Suite 2400; New York, NY 10036
(212) 997-1818; 997-1978 FAX
Peter Hagan, John Buzzetti, Scott Yoslow, Larry Tamb
Represents: Directors and Choreographers

Helen Merrill Ltd.
435 West 23rd St, Suite 1F; New York, NY 10011
(212) 691-5326; 727-0545 FAX
Beth Blickers, Patrick Herold, Morgan Jenness
Represents: Directors and Choreographers

International Creative Management
40 West 57th St; New York, NY 10019
(212) 556-5600; 556-5665 FAX
Sam Cohn, Paul Martino, Sarah Jane Leigh
Represents: Directors and Choreographers

Jack Lenny Associates
9454 Wilshire Blvd, #600; Beverly Hills, CA 90212
(310) 271-2174; 271-3540 FAX
and
100 West 57th St, #3I; New York, NY 10019
(212) 582-0270; 245-8099 FAX
Jack Lenny
Represents: Directors and Choreographers

Jerry Kahn, Inc.
853 7th Ave, #7C; New York, NY 10019
(212) 245-7317; 582-9898 FAX
Jerry Kahn
Represents:: Directors and Choreographers

The Joyce Ketay Agency
1501 Broadway, Suite 1908; New York, NY 10036
(212) 354-6825; 354-6732 FAX
Joyce P. Ketay, Carl Mulert, Wendy Streeter
Represents: Directors and Choreographers

Kazarian, Spencer & Associates
11365 Ventura Blvd, #100; Studio City, CA 91604
(818) 769-9111; 769-9847 FAX
Julie McDonald
Represents: Choreographers

Kerin, Goldberg & Associates, Inc.
155 East 55th St, Suite 5D; New York, NY 10022
(212) 838-7373; 838-0774 FAX
Charles Kerin
Represents: Directors and Choreographers

Lantz Agency
888 7th Ave, Suite 3001; New York, NY 10106
(212) 586-0200; 262-6659 FAX
Robert Lantz, Dennis Aspland
Represents: Directors

Pat Sullivan Management
315 East 86th St, Suite 2PE; New York, NY 10028
(212) 348-2770
Pat Sullivan
Represents: Directors

Peregrine Whittlesey
345 East 80th St, #31F; New York, NY 10021
(212) 737-0153; 734-5176 FAX
Peregrine Whittlesey
Represents: Directors

Peter Diggins
133 West 71st St, #8B; New York, NY 10023
(212) 874-4534; 874-4534 FAX
Peter Diggins
Represents: Directors and Choreographers for ballet and concert work

Professional Artists
513 West 54th St; New York, NY 10019
(212) 247-8770; 977-5686 FAX
Sheldon Lubliner, Marilynn Scott Murphy
Represents: Directors and Choreographers

Shukat Company, Ltd.
340 West 55th St, Suite 1A; New York, NY 10019
(212) 582-7614; 315-3752 FAX
Scott Shukat
Represents: Directors and Choreographers

Talent Representatives
20 East 53rd St, 2nd Floor; New York, NY 10022
(212) 752-1835; 752-7558 FAX
Honey Raider
Represents: Directors

The Tantleff Office
375 Greenwich St, Suite 700; New York, NY 10013
(212) 941-3939; 941-3948 FAX
Jack Tantleff
Represents: Directors and Choreographers

20th Century Artists
4605 Lankershim Blvd, Suite 305; North Hollywood, CA 91602
(818) 980-5118; 980-5449 FAX
Joe Ross
Represents: Directors and Choreographers

Waters & Nicolosi
1501 Broadway, Suite 1305; New York, NY 10036
(212) 302-8787; 382-1019 FAX
Jeanne Nicolosi
Represents: Directors and Choreographers

William Morris Agency
1325 Avenue of the Americas; New York, NY 10019
(212) 586-5100; 246-3583 FAX
George Lane, Samuel (Biff) Liff, Gilbert Parker, Johnnie Planco, Gene
Parseghian, Peter Franklin, Jason Fogelson
Represents: Directors and Choreographers

William Schill Agency
250 West 57th St, #2402; New York, NY 10107
(212) 315-5919; 397-7366 FAX
William Schill
Represents: Directors and Choreographers

Writers & Artists Agency
19 West 44th St, Suite 1000; New York, NY 10036
(212) 391-1112; 575-6397 (Literary FAX), 398-9877 (Talent FAX)
William Craver, Greg Wagner, Jeff Berger
Represents: Directors and Choreographers

ATTORNEYS

Agins, Siegal & Reiner
342 Madison Ave; New York, NY 10173
(212) 986-6166; 599-1281 FAX
Richard Agins
Represents: Directors and Choreographers

DaSilva & DaSilva
502 Park Ave, Suite 109; New York, NY 10022
(212) 752-9323; 421-4997 FAX
Albert I. DaSilva
Represents: Directors and Choreographers

Dumler & Giroux
575 Madison Ave; New York, NY 10022
(212) 759-4585; 751-1839 FAX
Egon Dumler
Represents: Directors and Choreographers

Elliot Brown, Esq.
488 Madison Ave; New York, NY 10022
(212) 935-5500; 308-0642 FAX
Elliot Brown, Esq.
Represents: Choreographers

Elliot J. Lefkowitz
641 Lexington Ave, 22nd Floor; New York, NY 10022
(212) 758-0860; 421-7983 FAX
Elliot J. Lefkowitz
Represents: Directors and Choreographers

Farber & Rich LLP
1370 6th Ave, 32nd Floor; New York, NY 10019
(212) 245-7777; 245-0594 FAX
Donald C. Farber
Represents: Directors and Choreographers

Fitelson, Lasky & Aslan
551 5th Ave, #614; New York, NY 10176
(212) 586-4700; 949-6746 FAX
Floria Lasky
Represents: Directors and Choreographers

Frankfurt, Garbus, Klein & Selz
488 Madison Ave, 9th Floor; New York, NY 10022
(212) 826-5534; 593-9175 FAX
Seth Gelblum
Represents: Directors and Choreographers

Gary N. DaSilva
616 Highland Ave; Manhattan Beach, CA 90266
(310) 318-5665; 318-2114 FAX
Gary N. DaSilva
Represents: Directors and Choreographers

Jay Kramer
135 East 55th St; New York, NY 10022
(212) 753-5420; 753-2546 FAX
Jay Kramer
Represents: Directors

Kay, Collyer & Boose
1 Dag Hammarskjold Plaza, 31st Floor; New York, NY 10017
(212) 940-8357; 755-0921 FAX
Jeremy Nussbaum
Represents: Directors and Choreographers

Leavy, Rosensweig, & Hyman
11 East 44th St; New York, NY 10017
(212) 983-0400; 983-2537 FAX
Scott Lazarus
Represents: Directors and Choreographers

Michael Lee Hertzberg, Esq.
740 Broadway, 5th Floor; New York, NY 10003
(212) 982-9870; 674-4614 FAX
Michael Lee Hertzberg
Represents: Directors and Choreographers

Moldover, Hertz, Cooper & Gidaly
750 3rd Ave, Suite 2400; New York, NY 10017
(212) 490-0100; 490-0124 FAX
Walter Gidaly
Represents: Directors and Choreographers

Pryor, Cashman, Sherman & Flynn
410 Park Ave, 10th Floor; New York, NY 10022
(212) 326-0150; 326-0806 FAX
Stephen Rodner, Esq.
Represents: Directors and Choreographers

Robinson, Brog, Leinwand, Reich, Genovese & Gluck, P.C.
1345 6th Ave, 36th Floor; New York, NY 10105
(212) 603-6308; 956-2164 FAX
Richard Ticktin, Esq., Roy A. Jacobs, Esq.
Represents: Directors and Choreographers

Sendroff & Associates
1500 Broadway, Suite 2001; New York, NY 10036
(212) 840-6400; 840-6401 FAX
Mark Sendroff
Represents: Directors and Choreographers

Solomon Glushak, Esq.
19 West 44th St; New York, NY 10036
(212) 730-1330; 768-1282 FAX
Solomon Glushak
Represents: Directors and Choreographers

Tanner, Propp LLP
99 Park Ave, 25th Floor; New York, NY 10016
(212) 986-7714; 687-0056 FAX
David G. Dubell
Represents: Directors

PERSONAL MANAGERS

The Cooper Company
2968 Corral Canyon Rd; Malibu, CA 90265
(310) 456-2351; 456-5703 FAX
Pamela Cooper
Represents: Directors and Choreographers

Davis Spylios Management
244 West 54th St, #707; New York, NY 10019
(212) 581-5766; 956-8789 FAX
Dale Davis, Harris Spylios
Represents: Directors and Choreographers

Nani-Saperstein Management
162 West 56th St, #307; New York, NY 10019
(212) 582-7690; 582-7785 FAX
Terry Saperstein
Represents: Directors and Choreographers

CHAPTER 7

REGIONAL THEATRE OPPORTUNITIES

R egional theatres offer many opportunities for directors and choreographers at various stages in their careers. Opportunities include internships, observerships, assistantships, fellowships and positions as contracted director or choreographer. The listings here include contact information, contract information and brief descriptions of opportunities offered.

Some theatres and artistic directors will accept unsolicited résumés and letters of interest; however many theatres specifically state that new directors or choreographers are hired through professional recommendation or observation of an artist's work. If a theatre is not interested in being contacted, we have also indicated that here. We recommend that you find out as much about a theatre as possible before contacting them. Find out what the particular theatre's season includes. Does the work they typically present match with the work that you do?

Three excellent companions to this chapter are Theatre Communications Group's Theatre Profiles 12, Theatre Directory and American Theatre magazine's October season preview issue. See our Books and Periodicals chapter for further information on these publications.

Sharon Ott, Artistic Director, Seattle Repertory Theatre; and Robert Moss, Artistic Director, Syracuse Stage, give advice on what to expect when working in a regional theatre.

REGIONAL THEATRE GUIDE

A Contemporary Theatre

Kreielsheimer Place; 700 Union St; Seattle, WA 98101
(206) 292-7660; 292-7670 FAX
E-mail: ad@act.iswnet.com
Web: http://www.acttheatre.org
Gordon Edelstein, Artistic Director

Contract: LORT C2. **Internships/Assistant Directors:** Unpaid. Assistant director positions for mainstage season Mar–Dec. Literary internships year-round. Contact the assistant to the artistic director. **Contracted Directors:** Through professional recommendation or observation of artist's work.

ACTheatre

Box 1454; Anniston, AL 36201
(205) 236-8342; 238-8364 FAX
E-mail: part22@aol.com
Douglas Millington, Managing Producer

Contract: Small Professional Theatre. **Internships:** Unpaid. Housing provided. **Contracted Directors:** Through professional recommendation or observation of artist's work.

Actors Theatre of Louisville

316–320 West Main St; Louisville, KY 40202-4218
(502) 584-1265; 561-3300 FAX
Web: http://www.actorstheatre.org
Jon Jory, Producing Director

Contracts: LORT B and D. **Internships:** Contact apprentice/internship director, Ms. Zan Sawyer-Dailey. **Contracted Directors/Choreographers:** Through professional recommendation and observation of artist's work by artistic director.

A.D. Players
2710 West Alabama; Houston, TX 77098
(713) 526-2721; 439-0905 FAX
E-mail: adplayers@hotmail.com
Web: http://www.adplayers.org
Jeanette C. George, Artistic Director

Internships: Available to those interested in becoming company members. A year of internship (with small stipend) is customary before membership. **Contracted Directors:** Through company affiliation or observation of artist's work by artistic director.

Alabama Shakespeare Festival
One Festival Dr; Montgomery, AL 36117-4605
(334) 271-5300; 271-5348 FAX
E-mail: pr4bard@wsnet.com
Web: http://www.asf.net/~pr4bard/asf.html
Kent Thompson, Artistic Director

Contracts: LORT C1 and D. **Internships/Observerships:** Available occasionally either through university program or individual basis. **Artistic Associates:** Through members of repertory company. **Contracted Directors/ Choreographers:** Through recommendation by artistic director or observation of artist's work.

Alliance Theatre Company
Robert W. Woodruff Arts Center; 1280 Peachtree St, NE; Atlanta, GA 30309
(404) 733-4650; 733-4625 FAX
Web: http://www.alliancetheatre.org
Kenny Leon, Artistic Director

Contracts: LORT B and D. **Internships/Observerships:** Contact Steve Lindsley for production internship application. Call observership hotline (404) 733-4708 for information and observership program application. **Contracted Directors:** Through observation of artist's work by artistic staff.

WHAT TO EXPECT
SHARON OTT, ARTISTIC DIRECTOR
SEATTLE REPERTORY THEATRE, SEATTLE, WASHINGTON

The experience of directing regionally will vary a great deal depending on the location of the theatre and it's budget. In general, the production standards are high, and the support staff is very good.

Once hired, directors may be asked to communicate their vision of the play to the Board of Directors and staff, as well as attend social events revolving around the theatre. Directors are sometimes expected to work with a certain number of local actors, but again, this depends on the budget of the theatre. Almost all LORT theatres offer housing (quality varies greatly depending on the city).

In larger cities, artistic directors will look for the best directing candidates locally. At Seattle Rep, we like to support artists from our community, if possible. Directors generally contact artistic directors via letters and a follow-up visit to the city. If a director piques my interest, I try to see a production he or she is directing, schedule permitting. It is good practice to let artistic directors know when you'll be directing, even if you are not in their area, because we often travel outside our area to see shows. It's important to get as many people as possible to see your work.

When working outside New York, the pay is generally fair and commensurate with the work. The salary will vary depending on which SSDC (Society of Stage Directors and Choreographers) contract the theatre uses. You can expect almost exactly the SSDC minimum negotiated contract amount, barring an unusually large project. Directors are rarely paid more than minimum unless they have returned to the theatre numerous times. Many directors start out directing in theatres classified as LORT D or lower, where the pay is considerably less than the larger theatres. However, once you are directing in LORT B houses and higher, the pay is quite reasonable.

American Conservatory Theater

30 Grant Ave, 6th Floor; San Francisco, CA 94108
(415) 834-3200; 834-3360 FAX
Web: http://www.act-sfbay.org
Carey Perloff, Artistic Director

Contract: LORT A. **Internships/Observerships:** Applications accepted each spring. Contact Susan West for information. **Contracted Directors:** Through enrollment in conservatory's student directing program, by professional referral or through observation of artist's work by artistic staff. Send résumé to artistic director.

American Showcase Theatre—Metrostage

1816 Duke St; Alexandria, VA 22314
(703) 548-9044; 548-9089 FAX
Carolyn Griffin, Producing Director

Contracted Directors/Choreographers: Through observation of artist's work by producing director.

Arena Stage

1101 6th Ave, SW; Washington, DC 20024
(202) 554-9066; 488-4056 FAX
E-mail: arenastg@shirenet.com
Web: http://www.arenastage.org
Molly D. Smith, Artistic Director

Contracts: LORT B+, B and D. **Internships/Fellowships:** Available on a per-show basis with weekly stipend. The Allen Lee Hughes Fellowship (See Chapter 4: Grants, Fellowships) for artists and administrators of color is a full-time position offered each season that requires a minimum 40-week commitment and offers a stipend of up to $10,000. Contact intern and fellows coordinator, A. Lorraine Robinson. **Contracted Directors:** Keep theatre informed of upcoming projects. The artistic director and associate producer will meet with directors visiting the Washington area.

GETTING TO KNOW YOU
ROBERT MOSS, ARTISTIC DIRECTOR
SYRACUSE STAGE, SYRACUSE, NEW YORK

At Syracuse Stage, we put together a season of seven shows, two of which I direct. There are one or two productions where a co-producing theatre hires the director. That leaves two or three openings per season. Sometimes a director whom I admire says to me, "Bob, I'm dying to do this play," and if I think it will work, I put it in the season. I try very hard to have those other slots filled by people whose work I know.

I think every artistic director would say the same thing when hiring a director: It's important to view his or her work. I always encourage young directors to let me know when they are doing projects, but not to be disappointed if I can't come. I'm only in New York City once a month.

In regional theatres, there is often a "meet and greet" on the first day of rehearsal, where the entire staff meets the director, the production staff and the actors. At Syracuse Stage, the visiting director meets the more than sixty people who are working not only on the current show, but on a season of shows. During the get-together, I ask the director why he or she is doing the play. This way the director gets a chance to talk about the piece with the entire staff, and get them excited. If the director has a facility for talking to groups, he or she is asked to speak at the local library, to community groups, or at talk-back sessions after a performance.

In Off-Broadway productions, the producer often comes in at the first preview and gives his or her feedback. In regional theatre, artistic directors usually get involved in the process. This is helpful because no one loses objectivity faster during rehearsals than a director.

I encourage an artistic director/director relationship, and try to be a helpful, friendly eye, and to not give oppressive notes. I will go into the rehearsal room because I love to watch other directors work, and I like to share my thoughts.

A guest director has to understand that regional theatres produce a body of work. There is a staff at Syracuse that is ongoing and devoted to the finest production of a play. Each director's production is crucially

continued on next page

important to all of us. At the same time, a director has to recognize that we have seven plays a season to produce. There are times when a director takes his or her frustrations out on the staff. Those directors are not invited back. We look for directors who work with grace under pressure. It's astonishing how simple it is to make it work: Respect the theatre's staff.

Arizona Theatre Company
Box 1631; Tucson, AZ 85702
(520) 884-8210; 628-9129 FAX
E-mail: atc@azstarnet.com
Web: http://www.aztheatreco.org
David Ira Goldstein, Artistic Director

Contract: LORT B. **Internships:** Contact assistant to the artistic director, Samantha Wyer. **Contracted Directors/Choreographers:** Direct solicitation by artistic director only.

Arrow Rock Lyceum Theatre
High St; Arrow Rock, MO 65320
(660) 837-3311
Michael Bollinger, Artistic Director

Contracts: LORT D and Letter of Agreement. **Internships:** Not available. **Contracted Directors/Choreographers:** On a regular basis, after observation of artist's work, through professional recommendation or through *Art-SEARCH* advertisement. (See Chapter 3: Books and Periodicals)

Asolo Theatre Company
5555 North Tamiami Trail; Sarasota, FL 34243
(941) 351-9010; 351-5796 FAX
Web: http://www.sarasota.online.com/asolo
Howard J. Millman, Producing Artistic Director

Contract: LORT C1. **Internships/Observerships:** Applications accepted each spring. Send letter and résumé to associate artistic director. **Contracted Directors:** Send letter of interest and résumé to the artistic director.

Bailiwick Repertory
1229 West Belmont; Chicago, IL 60657
(773) 883-1090; 525-3245 FAX
E-mail: bailiwick@aol.com
David Zak, Artistic Director

Contract: Chicago Area Theatre. **Internships:** Unpaid. On an individual basis. Send cover letter and résumé to managing director, Pat Acerra. **Contracted Directors/Choreographers:** Through Bailiwick's annual directors festival; artistic director also accepts letter of interest and résumé.

Barter Theatre
Box 867; Abingdon, VA 24212
(540) 628-2281; 628-4551 FAX
E-mail: barter@naxs.com
Richard Rose, Producing Artistic Director
John Hardy, Associate Artistic Director

Contract: LORT D. **Internships:** Call or write to the associate artistic director. **Observerships:** Usually arranged through MFA programs in local universities. Room is provided. **Artistic Associates:** Traditionally emerge from within company. **Contracted Directors/Choreographers:** Through observation of artist's work or professional recommendation.

Bay Street Theatre
Box 810; Sag Harbor, NY 11963
(516) 725-0818; 725-0906 FAX
E-mail: bayst@baystreet.org
Web: http://www.baystreet.org
Sybil Christopher, Emma Walton, Co-Artistic Directors

Contract: Letter of Agreement. **Assistant Directors:** Unpaid. Occasionally on an individual basis. **Contracted Directors:** At artistic directors' request with playwright's approval.

Berkeley Repertory Theatre
2025 Addison St; Berkeley, CA 94704
(510) 204-8901; 841-7711 FAX
E-mail: press@berkeleyrep.org
Web: http://www.berkeleyrep.org
Tony Taccone, Artistic Director

Contracts: LORT B and D. **Contracted Directors/Choreographers:** Relies on professional recommendations.

Berkshire Theatre Festival

Box 797; Stockbridge, MA 01262
(413) 298-5536; 298-3368 FAX
E-mail: info@berkshiretheatre.org
Web: http://www.berkshiretheatre.org/
Kate Maguire, Producing Director

Contract: LORT C1. **Artistic Associates:** Two available positions. **Contracted Directors:** Two productions by early-mid–career directors (5–6 years of professional experience) selected for summer festival. $1,500, pension, health benefits and room and board. Other director and choreographer positions are filled through professional recommendations from colleagues, such as The Drama League and Theatre Communications Group (See Chapter 5: Service Organizations).

Capital Repertory Theatre

111 North Pearl St; Albany, NY 12207
(518) 462-4531; 462-4531, ext. 293 FAX
E-mail: capitalrep@global2000.net
Web: http://www.capitalrep.org
Maggie Mancinelli-Cahill, Producing Artistic Director

Contract: LORT D. **Internships:** Full technical/production internship program available. **Contracted Directors/Choreographers:** Through professional recommendations.

Center Stage

700 North Calvert St; Baltimore, MD 21202
(410) 685-3200; 539-3912 FAX
E-mail: info@centerstage.org
Web: http://www.centerstage.org
Irene Lewis, Artistic Director

Contracts: LORT C1 and C2. **Internships:** Available through nearby college programs. **Contracted Directors/Choreographers:** Through observation and professional recommendation.

Chicago Dramatists

1105 West Chicago Ave; Chicago, IL 60622
(312) 633-0630; 633-0610 FAX
E-mail: newplays@aol.com
Russ Tutterow, Artistic Director

Contract: Chicago Area Theatre. **Contracted Directors:** Theatre solicits directors directly. No funds are available for hiring outside the Chicago area.

Childsplay, Inc.

Box 517; Tempe, AZ 85280
(602) 350-8101; 350-8584 FAX
E-mail: childsplayaz@juno.com
Web: http://www.tempe.gov/childsplay
David Saar, Artistic Director

Internships/Observerships: Most offered in connection with local state universities. **Contracted Directors/Choreographers:** Through professional recommendation from artistic directors.

Cincinnati Playhouse in the Park

Box 6537; Cincinnati, OH 45206
(513) 345-2242; 345-2254 FAX
E-mail: playhous@fuse.net
Web: http://www.cincyplay.com
Edward Stern, Producing Artistic Director

Contracts: LORT B and D. **Internships/Observerships:** Available through regional universities. **Contracted Directors/Choreographers:** Through observation of artist's work. Artistic director will meet with directors and choreographers if in the area.

The Cleveland Play House

Box 1989; Cleveland, OH 44106
(216) 795-7010; 795-7005 FAX
Web: http://www.cleveplayhouse.com
Peter Hackett, Artistic Director

Contracts: LORT B, C1 and D. **Internships/Observerships/Assistant Directors:** Available fall and spring. Internships are unpaid. **Artistic Associates:** Designated by the artistic director after significant contributions to the company. **Contracted Directors/Choreographers:** Staff directors and artistic associates often direct. Through professional recommendation and observation of artist's work by artistic director.

Crossroads Theatre Company
7 Livingston Ave; New Brunswick, NJ 08901
(732) 249-5581; 249-1861 FAX
Ricardo Khan, Co-Founder and Artistic Director

Contract: LORT D. **Observerships/Assistant Directors:** Theatre actively searches for new talent and encourages emerging directors and choreographers to contact them directly. Send letter and résumé to artistic director. **Contracted Directors/Choreographers:** Through professional recommendations from colleagues, such as Theatre Communications Group (See Chapter 5: Service Organizations) and professional playwrights.

Dallas Theater Center
3636 Turtle Creek Blvd; Dallas, TX 75219-5598
(214) 526-8210; 521-7666 FAX
Richard Hamburger, Artistic Director

Contract: LORT C1, C2 and D. **Internships:** Stipended positions available in directing/literary management for Aug–Apr season. Send résumé, three letters of recommendation and a letter of interest to artistic administrator, Alice Donohoe. **Contracted Directors:** Theatre actively searches for new directors whose work they find dynamic, original, intelligent and theatrical. The artistic team attends regional and New York productions often to broaden its knowledge of working directors.

Delaware Theatre Company
200 Water St; Wilmington, DE 19801
(302) 594-1104; 594-1107 FAX
E-mail: dtc@delawaretheatre.org
Web: http://www.delawaretheatre.org
Fontaine Syer, Artistic Director

Contract: LORT C2. **Internships/Observerships/Assistant Directing:** Available on an individual basis. **Contracted Directors:** Through professional recommendations or observation of artist's work.

Denver Center Theatre Company
1050 13th St; Denver, CO 80204
(303) 893-4000; 825-2117 FAX
E-mail: sellars@star.dcpa.org
Web: http://www.artstozoo.org/denvercenter
Donovan Marley, Artistic Director

Contracts: LORT B, C2 and D. **Contracted Directors:** Only in rare circumstances does theatre solicit new directors.

Florida Studio Theatre
1241 North Palm Ave; Sarasota, FL 34236
(941) 366-9017; 955-4137 FAX
Richard Hopkins, Artistic Director

Contracts: Small Professional Theatre. **Internships:** Available in directing and stage management. Interns earn points toward obtaining Actor's Equity status. Possible weekly stipend and free housing for the first year. Contact the intern coordinator. **Contracted Directors:** Submit cover letter and résumé to the company manager.

The Foothill Theatre Company
Box 1812; Nevada City, CA 95959
(530) 265-9320; 265-9325 FAX
E-mail: ftc@foothilltheatre.org
Web: http://www.foothilltheatre.org
Philip Charles Sneed, Artistic Director

Contracts: Small Professional Theatre, Guest Artist and Special Appearance. **Internships:** Available on an individual basis. **Contracted Directors:** Send résumé and cover letter to artistic director.

Foundation Theatre
Burlington County College; Route 530; Pemberton, NJ 08068
(609) 894-9311; 894-2801 FAX
Julie Ellen Prusinowski, Producing Director

Contract: 99-seat. **Internships/Observerships:** Contact producing director for application and interview. **Contracted Directors/Choreographers:** Through observation of artist's work or professional recommendation.

Free Street Programs
1419 West Blackhawk; Chicago, IL 60622
(773) 772-7248; 772-7248 FAX
E-mail: freest@mcs.net
Ron Bieganski, Artistic Director

Contract: Letter of Agreement. **Internships:** Unpaid positions with academic credit. **Contracted Directors:** Direct solicitation by artistic director only.

George Street Playhouse
9 Livingston Ave; New Brunswick, NJ 08901
(732) 846-2895; 247-9151 FAX
E-mail: twerder@georgestplayhouse.org
Web: http://georgestplayhouse.org
David Saint, Artistic Director

Contracts: LORT C2 and 99-seat. **Internships/Observerships/Assistant Directors:** Send letter of interest and résumé to the internship coordinator, Rachel Resinski. **Contracted Directors/Choreographers:** Through agent submission.

Geva Theatre
75 Woodbury Blvd; Rochester, NY 14607
(716) 232-1366; 232-4031 FAX
Web: http://www.gevatheatre.org
Mark Cuddy, Artistic Director

Contract: LORT B. **Internships:** Unpaid assistant director internships available. **Observerships:** Available through Theatre Communications Group (See Chapter 5: Service Organizations). **Assistant Directors:** Paid positions available for larger projects. **Contracted Directors/Choreographers:** Through observation of artist's work and professional recommendation. Theatre also accepts proposals.

The Goodman Theatre
200 South Columbus Dr; Chicago, IL 60603
(312) 443-3811; 263-6004 FAX
E-mail: staff@goodman-theatre.org
Web: http://www.goodman-theatre.org
Robert Falls, Artistic Director
Steve Scott, Associate Producer

Contracts: LORT B+ and D. **Internships/Assistant Directors:** Unpaid positons available. For an internship application contact the internship coordinator, Julie Massey. For assistant director positions, send letter of interest and résumé to associate producer. **Artistic Associates:** Available. **Contracted Directors/Choreographers:** Through observation of artist's work or professional recommendation from theatre personnel.

Goodspeed Opera House
Box A; East Haddam, CT 06423
(860) 873-8664; 873-2329 FAX
E-mail: mprice@goodspeed.org
Web: http://www.goodspeed.org
Michael P. Price, Executive Director

Contracts: LORT B and D. **Internships:** Contact internship coordinator, Sean Sullivan.

Great Lakes Theater Festival
1501 Euclid Ave, Suite 423; Cleveland, OH 44115
(216) 241-5490; 241-6315 FAX
James Bundy, Artistic Director

Contracts: LORT B. **Internships:** Assistant director/assistant to the artistic director internships available on a per show basis. Stipend, no housing.

The Group Theatre
305 Harrison St; Seattle, WA 98109
(206) 441-9480; 441-9839 FAX
José Carrasquillo, Artistic Director
Rex Carleton, Producing Director

Contracts: Small Professional Theatre and Theatre for Young Audiences. **Internships/Rehearsal Assistants/Associate Artists:** Emerging artists play a crucial role at the theatre. For production internships send letter and résumé to producing director. For administrative internships send letter and résumé to managing director, Donna Howell. **Contracted Directors:** Preference given to local artists, but occasionally will hire in.

Hartford Stage Company
50 Church St; Hartford, CT 06103
(860) 525-5601; 525-4420 FAX
Michael Wilson, Artistic Director

Contract: LORT B. **Internships/Observerships:** Send letter and résumé to artistic director. **Contracted Directors:** Through professional recommendation or observation of artist's work.

The Human Race Theatre Company
126 North Main St, Suite 300; Dayton, OH 45402-1710
(937) 461-3823; 461-7223 FAX
E-mail: hrtheatre@aol.com
Marsha Hanna, Artistic Director

Contract: Small Professional Theatre. **Internships:** Available through local university program. **Contracted Directors/Choreographers:** Through professional recommendation.

Huntington Theatre Company
264 Huntington Ave; Boston, MA 02115
(617) 266-7900; 353-8300 FAX
E-mail: htc@bu.edu
Web: http://www.bu.edu/huntington
Peter Altman, Producing Director

Contract: LORT B+. **Internships/Assistant Directors:** Not available. However, the producing director welcomes emerging artists to keep him informed about their work. **Contracted Directors:** The producing director conducts extensive scouting at professional theatre companies throughout the country, with particular emphasis on major theatre centers such as New York, Chicago, San Francisco and Seattle. Artists hired are those who have a body of work that demonstrates talent and professionalism, and shares Huntington's aesthetic.

Illinois Theatre Center
400A Lakewood Blvd; Park Forest, IL 60466
(708) 481-3510; 481-3693 FAX
E-mail: itcbillig@juno.com
Etel Billig, Producing Director

Contract: Chicago Area Theatre. **Internships/Assistant Directors:** Directing internships are available for Sept–Dec or Sept–May periods. Small stipend. Housing and transportation not provided. Prefers M.A. graduates. **Contracted Directors:** Through observation of artist's work. Artists may notify the producing director of upcoming productions.

Indiana Repertory Theatre
140 West Washington St; Indianapolis, IN 46204
(317) 635-5277; 236-0767 FAX
Web: http://www.indianarep.com
Janet Allen, Artistic Director

Contracts: LORT C1 and D. **Associate Artists:** By invitation only. **Contracted Directors:** Through observation of artist's work. Send letter and information regarding upcoming productions.

Intiman Theatre
Box 19760; Seattle, WA 98109-6645
(206) 269-1901; 269-1928 FAX
E-mail: intiman@intiman.org
Web: http://www.seattlesquare.com/intiman
Warner Shook, Artistic Director

Contract: LORT C2. **Internships:** Stipended journeymanships and unpaid internships available. Send letter and résumé to journeyman program coordinator. **Contracted Directors:** Through professional recommendation or observation of artist's work.

Jewish Repertory Theatre
92nd Street Y; 1395 Lexington Ave; New York, NY 10128
(212) 831-2001; 831-0082 FAX
E-mail: jrep@echonyc.com
Web: http://www.jrt.org
Ran Avni, Artistic Director

Contract: Letter of Agreement. **Internships/Assistant Directors:** Unpaid positions available each spring. Send letter and résumé to internship coordinator, Michael Lichtenstein. **Contracted Directors:** Through direct solicitation.

La Jolla Playhouse
Box 12039; La Jolla, CA 92039
(619) 550-1070; 550-1075 FAX
E-mail: ljplayhouse@ucsd.edu
Web: http://www.lajollaplayhouse.com
Michael Greif, Artistic Director

Contracts: LORT B and C2. **Observerships:** Occasionally. **Contracted Directors:** Through observation of artist's work or professional recommendation.

Lincoln Center Theater
150 West 65th St; New York, NY 10023
(212) 362-7600; 873-0761 FAX
Web: http://www.lct.org
André Bishop, Artistic Director

Contracts: LORT A and C2. **Emerging Artists:** Fifty to 100 unpaid directors chosen each spring for 3-week program consisting of workshops, symposiums, readings and discussions. For information and application write to the lab director, Anne Cattaneo. **Contracted Directors:** Through observation of artist's work.

Long Wharf Theatre
222 Sargent Dr; New Haven, CT 06511
(203) 787-4284; 776-2287 FAX
Web: http://www.longwharf.org
Douglas Hughes, Artistic Director

Contracts: LORT B and C2. **Internships:** Offered in all artistic, administrative and production departments. Stipend. Contact intern coordinator, Jeannette P. Lourde, for more information. **Contracted Directors:** Through agent submission, professional recommendation or observation.

Magic Theatre
Fort Mason Center, Building D; San Francisco, CA 94123
(415) 441-8001; 771-5505 FAX
E-mail: magicthtre@aol.com
Web: http://www.members.aol.com/magicthtre
Larry Eilenberg, Artistic Director

Contract: Bay Area Theatre. **Internships:** Send letter of interest to the artistic director. **Contracted Directors:** Send letter and résumé.

Manhattan Theatre Club
311 West 43rd St, 8th Floor; New York, NY 10036
(212) 399-3000; 399-4329 FAX
E-mail: questions@mtc-nyc.org
Web: http://www.mtc-nyc.org
Lynne Meadow, Artistic Director

Contract: Off-Broadway. **Internships/Assistant Directors:** Internships available in all departments year-round. Send résumés for unpaid assistant director positions; also accepts submissions from support organizations, such as The Drama League and Theatre Communications Group (See Chapter 5: Service Organizations). **Fellowships:** The Jonathan Alper Assistant Directorship for assistant directors on mainstage productions. Assistants receive a small stipend. Contact Jodi Simon Stewart, Artistic Associate. **Contracted Directors/ Choreographers:** Through agent submission or professional recommendation. Send letter and résumé.

Mark Taper Forum
135 North Grand Ave; Los Angeles, CA 90012
(213) 972-7353, 972-8051 FAX
Web: http://www.taper-ahmanson.com/ctg
Gordon Davidson, Artistic Director/Producer

Contracts: LORT A and 99-seat. **Internships:** Available through the New Work Festival. A 2–6 week (from Oct through Feb) internship provides an opportunity to observe all departments of the theatre as they produce workshops and readings of approximately 16 new works in a condensed period of time. Internships are available in three areas: Directing/Literary/Production Assistants; Producing; and Production Management. **Fellowships:** The Mellon Fellows Program for directors provides 2-year positions to mid-level directors, dramaturgs, artistic coordinators and/or producers. Fellows define his area of expertise and later take over the role of artistic director or producer. **Artis-**

tic Associates: By invitation only. **Contracted Directors/Choreographers:** Contact theatre for interview. Artistic staff actively searches in and out of the Southern California area for new talent.

McCarter Theatre Center for the Performing Arts
91 University Place; Princeton, NJ 08540
(609) 683-9100; 497-0369 FAX
E-mail: jwoodward@mccarter.org
Web: http://www.mccarter.org
Emily Mann, Artistic Director

Contracts: LORT B+ and D. **Internships/Observerships:** One directing intern accepted per season. Interns assigned as assistants to visiting and staff directors. There is a formal application process. Contact general manager, Kathleen Nolan. The McCarter hosts NEA and Drama League directors. **Observerships:** Available to Princeton University students. **Contracted Directors:** Through observation of artist's work. Staff producer, Mara Isaacs, meets with new directors by appointment.

Merrimack Repertory Theatre
Liberty Hall, 50 East Merrimack St; Lowell, MA 01852
(978) 454-6324; 934-0166 FAX
E-mail: mrtlowell@aol.com
Web: http://www.mrtlowell.com
David G. Kent, Producing Artistic Director

Contract: LORT D. **Internships/Assistant Directors:** Unpaid positions available. Send letter and résumé to the assistant to the artistic director, Emma Friend. **Contracted Directors:** Through professional recommendation from MRT associate only.

Mill Mountain Theatre
One Market Square SE, 2nd Floor; Roanoke, VA 24011-1437
(540) 342-5730; 342-5745 FAX
E-mail: MMTmail@intrlink.com
Web: http://www.intrlink.com/mmt
Jere Lee Hodgin, Producing Artistic Director

Contract: Guest Artist and Letter of Agreement. **Internships:** Usually unpaid position. Possible stipend and housing. Send letter of interest and résumé to internship coordinator year-round. **Contracted Directors:** Through professional recommendation. Occasionally hire new artists through ads in *Back Stage* or other industry publications.

Milwaukee Chamber Theatre
158 North Broadway; Milwaukee, WI 53202
(414) 276-8842; 277-4477 FAX
E-mail: mail@chamber-theatre.com
Web: http://www.chamber-theatre.com
Montgomery Davis, Artistic Director

Contract: Small Professional Theatre. **Internships:** Available through the Marquette University Theatre Department. **Contracted Directors/Choreographers:** Through professional recommendation or observation of artist's work.

Milwaukee Repertory Theatre
108 East Wells St; Milwaukee, WI 53202
(414) 224-1761; 224-9097 FAX
E-mail: milwaukeerep@aol.com
Joseph Hanreddy, Artistic Director

Contracts: LORT A, C1 and D. **Internships:** Unpaid positions available each Apr. Send letter of interest to the internship coordinator, Sandy Ernst. **Contracted Directors:** Through professional recommendation or observation. Send résumé and letter of interest to artistic director.

Missouri Repertory Theatre
4949 Cherry St; Kansas City, MO 64110
(816) 235-2727; 235-5367 FAX
E-mail: reecek@smtpgate.umkc.edu
George Keathley, Artistic Director

Contracts: LORT B and 99-seat. **Assistant Directors:** Unpaid positions available for 3–4 week periods. Send letter and résumé to artistic director. **Contracted Directors:** Through observation of artist's work by artistic director.

The Montana Repertory Theatre

Department of Drama/Dance; The University of Montana
Missoula, MT 59812-1582
(406) 243-6809; 243-5726 FAX
E-mail: mrt@selway.umt.edu
Web: http://www.umt.edu/mrt/mrt.html
Greg Johnson, Artistic Director

Contract: U/RTA. **Contracted Directors/Choreographers:** Available. Send cover letter and résumé.

New American Theater

118 North Main St; Rockford, IL 61101
(815) 963-9454; 963-7215 FAX
E-mail: bgregg@natc.net
Web: http://www.natc.net
William Gregg, Producing Artistic Director

Artistic Associates: Send cover letter and résumé to producing artistic director. **Contracted Directors/Choreographers:** Through professional recommendation and observation of artist's work.

New Jersey Shakespeare Festival

36 Madison Ave; Madison, NJ 07940
(973) 408-3278; 408-3361 FAX
E-mail: njsf@njshakespeare.org
Web: http://www.njshakespeare.org
Bonnie J. Monte, Artistic Director

Contracts: Small Professional Theatre and Letter of Agreement. **Internships/Observerships:** Available for directors and teachers. Arranged by an application and interview process conducted through the artistic and education offices. **Contracted Directors/Choreographers:** Hired on a per-show basis. Through the application and interview process, from professional recommendations and through NJSF's training program. Send cover letter and résumé to artistic director.

New York State Theatre Institute
155 River St; Troy, NY 12180
(518) 274-3200; 274-3815 FAX
E-mail: nysti@crisny.org
Web: http://www.crisny.org/not-for-profit/nysti
Patricia Di Benedetto Snyder, Producing Artistic Director

Contract: Theatre for Young Audiences. **Internships:** Contact intern administrator, Arlene Leff. **Contracted Directors/Choreographers:** Through professional recommendation or observation of artist's work.

New York Theatre Workshop
79 East 4th St; New York, NY 10003
(212) 780-9037; 460-8996 FAX
E-mail: NYTW@aol.com
James C. Nicola, Artistic Director

Contract: Letter of Agreement. **Internships/Assistant Directors:** Available year-round. Small stipend for full-time interns. Send letter and résumé to associate artistic director. **Contracted Directors:** Send résumé; also through observation of artist's work or agent recommendation.

Northlight Theatre
North Shore Center for the Performing Arts in Skokie;
9501 North Skokie Blvd; Skokie, IL 60076
E-mail: ntheatre@aol.com
Web: http://www.northlight.org
(847) 679-9501; 679-1879 FAX
B. J. Jones, Artistic Director

Contract: LORT D. **Internships:** Unpaid positions available in administration, production and artistic direction. Contact the artistic associate. **Contracted Directors:** Through observation of artist's work.

Old Globe Theatre
Box 2171; San Diego, CA 92112-2171
(619) 231-1941; 231-5879 FAX
E-mail: oldglobe@oldglobe.org
Web: http://www.oldglobe.org
Jack O'Brien, Artistic Director

Contracts: LORT B, B+ and C2. **Internships:** Contact theatre.

Olney Theatre Center for the Arts
2001 Olney-Sandy Spring Rd; Olney, MD 20832
(301) 924-4485; 924-2654 FAX
Jim A. Petosa, Artistic Director

Contract: COST minimum. **Contracted Directors/Choreographers:** Send cover letter and résumé to the producing director.

Oregon Shakespeare Festival
Box 158; Ashland, OR 97520
(541) 482-2111, ext. 293; 482-0446 FAX
E-mail: timb@orshakes.org
Web: http://www.orshakes.org
Timothy Bond, Associate Artistic Director

Contract: LORT IPA-B+. **Assistant Directors:** Offers a graduate directing assistantship for M.F.A. graduate directing students who are looking for professional assistant directing opportunities for college credit during their final year of study. The assistant director works on two large-scale productions over a two-month residency. Housing is provided.

Pacific Alliance Stage Company
Speckels Performing Arts Center; 5409 Snyder Lane;
Rohnert Park, CA 94928
(707) 586-0936; 586-9030 FAX
Michael Grice, Artistic Director

Contracted Directors/Choreographers: Through professional recommendation and observation of artist's work. Send résumé.

People's Light and Theatre Company
39 Conestoga Rd; Malvern, PA 19355
(610) 647-1900; 640-9521 FAX
E-mail: plt@msn.com
Abigail Adams, Artistic Director

Contract: LORT D. **Internships:** Available. Small stipend and housing. Send letter and résumé to the artistic director. **Contracted Directors/Choreographers:** Through observation. Send résumé and letter of interest to the artistic director.

Perseverance Theatre
914 3rd St; Douglas, AK 99824
(907) 364-2421; 364-2603 FAX
E-mail: persthr@ptialaska.net
Web: http://www.juneau.com/pt/
Peter DuBois, Artistic Director

Internships: Available in directing, acting, production, administration and writing. Three to 5 month periods. Monthly stipend. The theatre hires primarily Alaskan residents. Contact the training director. **Contracted Directors/Choreographers:** Hired on a per-show basis.

Philadelphia Theatre Company
The Belgravia; 1811 Chestnut St, Suite 300; Philadelphia, PA 19103
(215) 568-1920; 568-1944 FAX
E-mail: ptcnet@aol.com
Web: http://www.phillytheatreco.com
Sara E. Garonzik, Producing Artistic Director

Contract: LORT D. **Internships:** Available for mainstage productions. Small stipend. **Contracted Directors/Choreographers:** Through observation of artist's work by producing artistic director in Philadelphia/New Jersey, New York and Louisville regions; and through professional recommendation of agent and artistic directors.

Ping Chong and Company
47 Great Jones St; New York, NY 10012
(212) 529-1557; 529-1703 FAX
E-mail: 103034.434@compuserve.com
Ping Chong, Artistic Director

Internships/Observerships: Available. Call for information. **Contracted Directors:** Through direct solicitation only.

Pirate Playhouse
Box 1459; Sanibel, FL 33957
(813) 472-4109; 472-0055 FAX
E-mail: pirateplay@aol.com
Robert Kalfin, Artistic Director

Contract: Small Professional Theatre. **Contracted Directors/Choreographers:** Through observation of artist's work. Theatre also places advertisements in *ArtSEARCH* and *Back Stage*. (See Chapter 3: Books and Periodicals.)

Pittsburgh Public Theater
6 Allegheny Square; Pittsburgh, PA 15212-5349
(412) 323-8200; 323-8550 FAX
E-mail: pittpublic@aol.com
Web: http://www.pghpublictheater.org
Edward Gilbert, Artistic Director

Contract: LORT C1. **Internships/Observerships:** Offered through Carnegie Mellon Graduate Arts Management Program. **Contracted Directors/Choregraphers:** Through professional recommendation and observation of artist's work.

PlayMakers Repertory Company
CB #3235 Graham Memorial, Bldg 052A; Chapel Hill, NC 27599-3235
(919) 962-1122; 962-4069 FAX
E-mail: murf@email.unc.edu
Web: http://www.playmakers.org
Milly S. Barranger, Producing Director

Contract: LORT D. **Internships:** No formal program exists, but internships can be arranged by contacting the director with whom the intern wishes to study. **Contracted Directors:** Direct solicitation only.

Portland Center Stage
Box 9008; Portland, OR 97207
(503) 248-6309; 769-6509 FAX
E-mail: Cynthia@pcs.org
Web: http://www.pcs.org
Elizabeth Huddle, Artistic Director

Contract: LORT B. **Contracted Directors:** Through direct solicitation and observation of artist's work.

Portland Stage Company
Box 1458; Portland, ME 04104
(207) 774-1043; 774-0576 FAX
E-mail: portstage@aol.com
Anita Stewart, Artistic Director

Contract: LORT D. **Internships:** Available. $100 stipend. Call theatre for application and brochure. **Contracted Directors:** Through professional recommendation or observation of artist's work.

Primary Stages
584 Ninth Ave; New York, NY 10036
(212) 333-7471; 333-2025 FAX
E-mail: primary@ix.netcom.com
Casey Childs, Artistic Director
Seth Gordon, Associate Producer

Contract: Letter of Agreement. **Internships/Observerships/Assistant Directors:** Unpaid positions available for work on new play production. Send letter and résumé to the associate producer. **Contracted Directors:** Through professional recommendation.

The Rose Theater
2001 Farnham; Omaha, NE 68102
(402) 345-4852; 344-7255 FAX
James Larson, Artistic Director

Artistic Associates: Hired. Contact artistic director. **Contracted Directors:** Direct solicitation by theatre.

Roundabout Theatre Company
1530 Broadway; New York, NY 10036
(212) 719-9393; 869-8817 FAX
E-mail: stephen@www.roundabouttheatre.org
Web: http://www.roundabouttheatre.org
Todd Haimes, Artistic Director

Contract: LORT B+. **Internships:** Available in casting and stage management only. Contact education director, Margaret Salvante. **Assistant Directors:** Brought to the theatre by the director of each production. **Artistic Associates:** Hired after an extended association with the theatre. **Contracted Directors:** Through direct solicitation by artistic director.

Sacramento Theatre Company
1419 H St; Sacramento, CA 95814
(916) 446-7501; 446-4066 FAX
Stephen Rothman, Artistic Director
Ernest A. Figueroa, Associate Artistic Director

Contracts: LORT D and Letter of Agreement. **Internships/Observerships/Assistant Directors:** Unpaid positions available each spring typically through local university graduate school for credit. Send letter and résumé to associate artistic director. **Contracted Directors/Choreographers:** Directors may send résumés, followed by professional recommendation. Theatre mostly books in shows. Choreographers are typically contracted locally.

San Jose Repertory Theatre
101 Paseo de San Antonio; San Jose, CA 95113
(408) 291-2266; 367-7237 FAX
Web: http://www.sjrep.com
Timothy Near, Artistic Director

Contract: LORT C1. **Contracted Directors/Choreographers:** Through professional recommendation or observation.

Seacoast Repertory Theatre
125 Bow St; Portsmouth, NH 03801
(603) 433-4793; 431-7818 FAX
E-mail: srt@genitech.com
Web: http://www.seacoastrep.org
Roy M. Rogosin, Founder/Producing Artistic Director

Contracts: Guest Artist and Special Appearance. **Internships/Observerships:** Send résumé and bio. **Fellowships:** Available on a case-by-case basis only. **Contracted Directors/Choreographers:** Through direct solicitation by producing artistic director.

Seaside Music Theatre
Box 2835; Daytona Beach, FL 32120
(904) 252-3394; 252-8991 FAX
E-mail: smthead@aol.com
Herbert M. Davidson, Jr., Producer

Observerships/Rehearsal Assistants: Through Florida State University or the University of Florida. **Contracted Directors:** Through professional recommendation.

Seattle Repertory Theatre
155 Mercer St; Seattle, WA 98109
(206) 443-2210; 443-2379 FAX
Web: http://www.seattlerep.org
Sharon Ott, Artistic Director

Contracts: LORT B+ and D. **Internships:** Two full-time (40 hours per week) internships per season are available through "The Professional Arts Training

Program." Small stipend; housing is not provided. Contact the intern coordinator. **Contracted Directors:** Send résumé, two professional recommendations and letter of interest to the artistic staff.

Second Stage Theatre
Box 1807 Ansonia Station; New York, NY 10023
(212) 787-8302; 877-9886 FAX
E-mail: s2ndstage@aol.com
Carole Rothman, Artistic Director

Contract: Letter of Agreement. **Internships/Assistant Directors:** Hired for most shows. Year-long paid fellowships program for young (under 30) minority directors. Contact the literary manager. **Contracted Directors/Choreographers:** Through observation of artist's work by artistic director or professional recommendation.

The Shakespeare Theatre
301 East Capitol St, SE; Washington, DC 20003
(202) 547-3230, 547-0226 FAX
E-mail: MichaelK@shakespearedc.org
Web: http://www.shakespearedc.org
Michael Kahn, Artistic Director

Contract: LORT B. **Internships/Observerships/Assistant Directors:** Two paid positions are available: assistant director and resident directorial assistant. These positions are open to the general public and are posted when they become available in various publications and in theatre's Web Site. **Contracted Directors/Choreographers:** Through direct solicitation by artistic director or by agent submission.

South Coast Repertory
Box 2197, 655 Town Center Drive; Costa Mesa, CA 92628
(714) 708-5500; 545-0391 FAX
E-mail: theatre@scr.org
Web: http://www.ocartsnet.org/scr/
Martin Benson, Artistic Director

Contracts: LORT B and D. **Internships/Observerships:** Available. For information contact artistic associate, Nancy Herman. **Artistic Associates:** Hired. **Contracted Directors/Choreographers:** Send résumé and letter of interest.

Syracuse Stage
820 East Genesee St; Syracuse, NY 13210-1508
(315) 443-4008; 443-9846 FAX
E-mail: rhmoss@mailbox.syr.edu
Web: http://www.syracusestage.org
Robert Moss, Artistic Director

Contracts: LORT C1 and Theatre for Young Audiences. **Internships/ Observerships:** Available to directing graduate students in the Department of Drama at Syracuse Stage. **Contracted Directors/Choreographers:** Through observation of artist's work and interview by artistic director. Send information on upcoming productions to theatre.

Tennessee Repertory Theatre
427 Chestnut St; Nashville, TN 37203
(615) 244-4878; 244-1232 FAX
E-mail: tnrep@isdn.net
Web: http://www.therep.hammock.com
Mac Pirkle, Artistic Director

Contract: LORT C+. **Contracted Directors/Choreographers:** Through professional recommendation from theatres and service organizations, such as the National Alliance for Musical Theatre (NAMT) (See Chapter 5: Service Organizations), since TRT often produces musicals.

Theater Emory
Emory University; Atlanta, GA 30322
(404) 727-0524; 727-6253 FAX
E-mail: vmurphy@emory.edu
Web: http://www.emory.edu/ARTS/
Vincent Murphy, Artistic Producing Director

Contract: Small Professional Theatre. **Internships:** Available to students at Emory University. **Fellowships:** Available. Possible small stipend if in residence. **Contracted Directors/Choreographers:** Through observation of artist's work or professional recommendation.

Theatre for a New Audience
154 Christopher St, Suite 3D; New York, NY 10014-2839
(212) 229-2819; 229-2911 FAX
Web: http://www.tfana.com
Jeffrey Horowitz, Artistic Director

Contract: LORT D. **Internships/Assistant Directors:** Honorariums for 1 or 2 assistant directors per season; honorariums for assistant to the artistic director also available. Send inquiries by mail only to the attention of the general manager. **Contracted Directors/Choreographers:** Through direct solicitation only. Do not contact theatre.

Theater of the First Amendment
George Mason University; Institute of the Arts; Mail Stop 3E6;
Fairfax, VA 22030-4444
(703) 993-2195; 993-2191 FAX
E-mail: rdavi4@osfl.gmu.edu
Web: http://www.web.gmu.edu/cfa
Rick Davis, Artistic Director

Contract: Letter of Agreement. **Contracted Directors:** Send specific project proposals and general expressions of interest to artistic director. Experience in working with contemporary or new plays is a key factor in hiring.

TheatreVirginia
2800 Grove Ave; Richmond, VA 23221
(804) 353-6100; 353-8799 FAX
E-mail: tva@erols.com
Web: http://www.web.theatreva.com
George Black, Producing Artistic Director

Contract: LORT C1. **Internships/Observerships/Assistant Directors:** Unpaid positions awailable; some with academic credit. Send letter and résumé to director of education and outreach, Ms. Elan Connor. Graduate level internships available through Professional Track Directing Program of Virginia Commonwealth University. **Contracted Directors/Choreographers:** Through professional recommendation only.

Trinity Repertory Company
201 Washington St; Providence, RI 02903
(401) 521-1100; 521-0447 FAX
E-mail: info@trinityrep.com
Web: http://www.trinityrep.com
Oskar Eustis, Artistic Director

Contracts: LORT C1 and D. **Internships/Observerships:** Available. Contact Neil Bavan, ext. 226. **Contracted Directors/Choreographers:** Through observation by artistic director.

Virginia Stage Company
Box 3770; Norfolk, VA 23514
(757) 627-6988; 628-5958 FAX
Web: http://www.whro.org/cl/vsc
Charlie Hensley, Artistic Director
Kenton Yeager, Associate Artistic Director

Contracts: LORT C1 and 99-seat. **Internships/Observerships:** Available. Contact associate artistic director. **Contracted Directors/Choreographers:** Artistic director meets with directors or choreographers who travel to Norfolk and interviews when in New York City. Send résumé and letter of interest.

The Walnut Street Theatre Company
825 Walnut St; Philadelphia, PA 19107
(215) 574-3550; 574-3598 FAX
Bernard Havard, Producing Artistic Director

Internships/Assistant Directors: Unpaid positions available. Academic credit. **Apprenticeships:** Available in the literary or stage management departments. **Contracted Directors/Choreographers:** Send project proposals to producing artistic director.

West Coast Ensemble
c/o The Wald Organization; 2422 Wilshire Blvd, Suite A;
Santa Monica, CA 90403
(310) 449-1447; 829-6776 FAX
Les Hanson, Artistic Director

Contract: 99-seat. **Contracted Directors:** Those interested in becoming members of the ensemble should send a letter of introduction and a résumé to the attention of the Directors Lab.

White River Theatre Festival
Box 336; White River Junction, VT 05001
(802) 295-6221
Stephen Legawiec, Artistic Director

Contracted Directors/Choreographers: Directors hired through observation. Keep theatre informed of upcoming productions. Choreographers should submit letter of inquiry and be prepared to submit videotape should theatre ask.

The Wilma Theater
265 South Broad St; Philadelphia, PA 19107
(215) 893-9456; 893-0895 FAX
E-mail: wilma@libertynet.org
Web: http://wilmatheater.org
Blanka Zizka and Jiri Zizka, Artistic Producing Directors

Contract: LORT D. **Internships:** Year-round unpaid positions. **Fellowships:** Paid positions. Application deadline is in May. Call Char Vandermoor, ext. 101, for application guidelines. **Contracted Directors/Choreographers:** Send résumé and letter of interest to the artistic director.

Women's Project & Productions
55 West End Ave; New York, NY 10023
(212) 765-1706; 765-2024 FAX
E-mail: wpp@earthlink.net
Web: http://www.women'sproject.org
Julia Miles, Artistic Director

Contact: Letter of Agreement. **Mentoring Opportunities:** Positions through the "Directors Forum" and/or assistantships to directors. **Contracted Directors/Choreographers:** Through mentoring programs or professional recommendation from playwright.

Woolly Mammoth Theatre Company
1401 Church St, NW; Washington, DC 20005
(202) 234-6130; 667-0904 FAX
E-mail: woollymamm@aol.com
Howard Shalwitz, Artistic Director

Contract: Small Professional Theatre. **Internships:** Available. Contact Molly White for information. **Contracted Directors:** Through observation of artist's work by artistic director.

Yale Reptertory Theatre
Box 208244; 222 York St; New Haven, CT 06520
(203) 432-1515; 432-8332 FAX
Web: http://www.yale.edu/drama
Stan Wojewodski, Jr., Artistic Director

Contracts: Lort C and C1. **Contracted Directors/Choreographers:** Through direct solicitation and professional recommendation.

CHAPTER 8

PRODUCING YOUR OWN WORK

ORGANIZATIONS THAT SERVE NOT-FOR-PROFIT AND COMMERCIAL PRODUCTIONS

Producing one's own work poses challenges that a director or choreographer may not otherwise encounter. For this reason, we present many perspectives on producing—from producing the single theatrical event to forming a theatre company. We've included discussions on the role of the press agent, by Jeffrey Richards, and the role of the general manager, by Marshall B. Purdy of Walt Disney Theatricals. W. E. Scott Hoot, Esq., formerly with Volunteer Lawyers for the Arts, describes the fundamental differences between a not-for-profit and commercial approach to producing. Jeremy Dobrish, Artistic Director of adobe Theatre Company, Douglas Carter Beane, Artistic Director of The Drama Dept. and Claudia Catania, Executive Producer of The New Group, tell the stories of the birth and development of each of their respected theatre companies. Also included in this chapter is a list of organizations that serve the not-for-profit and/or commercial producer. Listings are in alphabetical order, by name of organization, and contain address information and a brief description of the organization. For further information on dues and eligibility, contact each organization directly.

Alliance of Resident Theatres/New York
131 Varick St, Room 904; New York, NY 10013
(212) 989-5257; 989-4880 FAX
E-mail: artnewyork@aol.com
Virginia P. Louloudes, Executive Director

When developing your not-for-profit theatre company, ART/New York has many programs that can be helpful. The Nancy Quinn Fund provides technical assistance, workshops and cash awards to small and emerging companies. If you are looking for space, check out the Elizabeth Steinway Chapin Real Estate Loan Fund. (See Chapter 5: Service Organizations.)

Asian American Arts Alliance
74 Varick St, Suite 302; New York, NY 10013-1914
(212) 941-9208; 941-7978 FAX
E-mail: aaaajc@pipeline.com
Lillian Cho, Executive Director

Two programs that assist Asian-American companies are Technical Assistance and Regrant Initiative (TARI), which helps New York City groups with administrative issues; and Presenting Opportunities Pilot (POP), which gives artistic assistance. (See Chapter 5: Service Organizations.)

Association of Hispanic Arts
250 West 26th St, 4th Floor; New York, NY 10001
(212) 727-7227; 727-0549 FAX
E-mail: aha96@aol.com
Sandra M. Perez, Executive Director

New not-for-profit Hispanic companies can benefit from AHA's financial management systems and planning assistance. Technical assistance is also available. (See Chapter 5: Service Organizations.)

Black Theatre Network
2603 Northwest 13th St, Suite 312; Gainesville, FL 32609
(352) 495-2116; 495-2051 FAX
E-mail: manicho@aol.com
Mikell Pinkney, President

At BTN's national forums, new theatre companies can network and seek advice of other artists and administrators. (See Chapter 5: Service Organizations.)

MAKING ADOBE THEATRE COMPANY
JEREMY DOBRISH, ARTISTIC DIRECTOR
ADOBE THEATRE COMPANY, NEW YORK CITY

I started the adobe Theatre Company in 1991 with a bunch of friends who had all gone to school together. We thought it would be empowering to do the projects we wanted to do, and continue in the collaborative way that we had at Wesleyan. For my own training, I got a job at Soho Rep, and learned everything I needed in terms of producing in New York City. I was at Soho Rep for about three years, and about six months into that I started adobe. We used the Soho Rep space to perform for about six years.

At the very beginning, we really had no money, and we couldn't afford to rent the space. Soho Rep allowed us to produce when the space was not being used. We would get a phone call: "Six weeks from now we have two weeks available, do you want it?" We'd say, "Great!" And, we'd throw together a show in six weeks. That's a terrible way to do it. Eventually as our budget grew we were able to say, "No, we don't want it in six weeks, but we've got this project that we want to do in two or three months, and we'll pay for it."

We went the not-for-profit route right away. If you're going for-profit, the only people going to give you money are those who think they're going to make their money back. Most theatre at this level doesn't make money, so nobody's going to give you money as an investment—they'll give it as a donation. If it's a tax-deductible donation (as many not-for-profit arts donations are), so much the better. We were also eligible for grants. But we knew that getting grants was extremely difficult—it's very competitive and the money is drying up.

For us it really took a while to get going. It's hard to get reviewers to come see you when you don't have a name, when you're not a proven quantity. But eventually they came, and they were very kind. That helped tremendously.

When we started, we were young and very naive, and we just sort of jumped in and did it. It was through actually doing it that we developed our own style and our own taste. Now we can say, "This is what adobe does, and we do it well." We've also grown. We started with six people, and now there are twenty-five. We picked up like-minded artists along the way.

Business Resource & Investment Service Center
271 West 125th St, Room 215; New York, NY 10027
(212) 866-5640; 866-7607 FAX
Herman Velazquez, Executive Director

BRISC, a joint project of the Upper Manhattan Empowerment Zone Development Corporation and the U.S. Small Business Administration, provides comprehensive business advice and access to financial assistance. BRISC brings together existing providers of small business assistance and financing in a centralized location.

The Commercial Theatre Institute
250 West 57th St, Suite 1818; New York, NY 10107
(212) 586-1109; 581-9373 FAX
Frederic B. Vogel, Director

CTI is a project of the Theatre Development Fund (TDF) and The League of American Theatres and Producers. CTI serves as both an informational source and a forum for illuminating the various paths one can take in creating commercial productions. A major objective of CTI is the investigation of the relationship between the for-profit and the not-for-profit sectors in project development. CTI currently maintains two programs: the Three-Day Program is open to anyone interested in producing, co-producing or investing in the commercial theatre—Broadway, Off-Broadway, tours and Sit-Down productions (commercial productions with open runs). This program, conducted every April/May, is composed of panels of producers, general managers, entertainment attorneys and managing directors. The Fourteen-Week Program is designed to present in-depth information, insight and planning for various aspects of producing in the commercial arena. Sessions, scheduled for fourteen consecutive Monday nights, provide for discussions and interaction with working professionals in the commercial theatre. This program is limited to twenty-five participants, who must be nominated by a working member of the professional theatrical community. Nominations are solicited every October/November.

Florida Professional Theatres Association
Box 2922; West Palm Beach, FL 33402-2922
(561) 848-6231; 848-7291 FAX
E-mail: kaizen21@aol.com
Sherron Long, Manager

An association of Florida's professional theatres and theatre professionals, FPTA conducts annual statewide auditions for Equity and non-Equity actors,

MAKING THE DRAMA DEPT.
DOUGLAS CARTER BEANE, ARTISTIC DIRECOR
DRAMA DEPT., NEW YORK CITY

A few years ago, a theatre company had a retreat at which one of my
works was read. I went there with some actors who were taking
part, among them the actress, Cynthia Nixon.

During the ride home we talked. We both felt we didn't have much
of a say in our careers. I was frustrated, she was frustrated. At the end
of that conversation we stated: "If we had a theatre company, it would
be a collective for artists to do their work, the way they want to do it.
Any artist—even a designer—could start a project."

The next day, Cynthia called me. "Were you serious about that?"
she asked. I said, "Yes, I think I am." Cynthia said, "I don't want to be
the teenage girl who's sitting by the phone waiting for the call. I want
to be the teenage girl who *makes* the call." So we just started calling our
friends, all of whom felt the same way. They were in the same place in
their careers. They wanted to do film and TV to make money, and then
come back and do a play. This is the life of most theatre people today.

We thought, "Wouldn't it be great if we were in control? If we could
produce the works we wanted, decide what movies we would do, and
make movies out of the plays we produced?" Then we tried to make it
all happen. That's how the Drama Dept. got started.

We didn't produce for two years—we spent all of that time reading
through plays and trying to figure out what we were going to be. Today,
we still get together every week and read through a play, old or new, and
talk about it. By the time we start work on it, everyone has a stake in it.

The money part was tough. But I had a successful film credit under
my belt, so I went to film studios and basically said, "I'm starting this
theatre company—why don't you give me some money?" I ended up
with a deal in which New Line, Fine Line, agreed to produce four new
plays for us, and I gave them first refusal of the screen rights.

The deal amounts to a nice chunk of change, and Fine Line doesn't
have any say in what we write. With writers like Nicky Silver and Peter
Hedges in the company, who knows what the material's going to be.

continued on next page

MAKING THE DRAMA DEPT. CONTINUED

There's no controlling those two. But, even with successful writers and a decent track record, it's very tough to find people willing to invest in the company. We always have problems paying for the Xeroxing of scripts, organizing readings and getting scripts to people.

We put together our board of directors in very much the same way we put the company together: "Who do we know? Do we like their work? What are they like?" I went to people I had worked with—general managers, producers, entertainment lawyers—all who knew the business end of things, people who had worked with not-for-profit companies before. Today, we continue to look for other people to come on board and guide us in this way.

No one is looking to make their name with our company. Billy Crudup doesn't need to do a play with us to get a big part in a movie. Everyone is doing it to *do it*. Everyone is busy—people get other jobs—and this is the tough part. But what encourages me is that every Thursday in my living room there are people reading scripts—still working. It's been the best professional experience of my life.

---

holds workshops, publishes a newsletter, maintains a professional job-bank file and a statewide audition and job hotline (561-840-9771) for theatre professionals, and serves as a clearinghouse for information about professional theatre in Florida.

The Foundation Center
79 Fifth Ave; New York, NY 10003-3076
(212) 620-4230, (800) 424-9836; (212) 691-1828 FAX
Web: http://www.fdncenter.org
Sara L. Engelhardt, President

New not-for-profit theatre companies can benefit from the Center's extensive library of information on not-for-profit management and fundraising. (See Chapter 4: Grants, Funding.)

Institute of Outdoor Drama
University of North Carolina;
CB3240 Nations Bank Plaza, Suite 201; Chapel Hill, NC 27599-3240
(919) 962-1328; 962-4212 FAX
E-mail: outdoor@unc.edu
Web: http://www.unc.edu/depts/outdoor/
Scott J. Parker, Director

For outdoor theatres, the Institute can provide a wide range of services, including feasibility studies for outdoor drama projects, a national conference, national auditions and a quarterly newsletter. (See Chapter 5: Service Organizations.)

The League of American Theatres and Producers
226 West 47th St; New York, NY 10036-1487
(212) 764-1122; 719-4389 FAX
E-mail: league@broadway.org
Web: http://www.broadway.org
Jed Bernstein, Executive Director

The League is the professional trade association of the taxpaying legitimate theatre. Its national membership includes producers, theatre owners and operators, and local presenters. The League's programs include labor relations and negotiations; marketing, economic and media research; audience development; urban environment improvement; government relations; publications; institutional public relations and promotion; tourism promotion; education programs; and presentation of the Tony Awards with the American Theatre Wing.

League of Chicago Theatres/League of Chicago Theatres Foundation
228 South Wabash, Suite 300; Chicago, IL 60604
(312) 554-9800; 922-7202 FAX
E-mail: theleague@aol.com
Web: http://www.theaterchicago.org
Marj Halperin, Executive Director

The League is an association of producers and theatres which promotes the advancement of the theatre industry in Chicago, by providing marketing, advocacy and informational services to its members. Programs include HOTTIX half- and full-price ticket centers, cooperative advertising, publications and cross-cultural auditions. The Foundation, the fundraising arm of the league, works to support, enhance and advance programs of the league.

THE PRESS AGENT
JEFFREY RICHARDS, PRESS AGENT
JEFFREY RICHARDS ASSOCIATES, NEW YORK CITY

When should the press agent become involved in a show? Ideally, when the producer has the vision that he is going to do a particular project, and wants to start a buzz.

I belong to a union which is called the Association of Theatrical Press Agents and Managers (ATPAM). According to union rules, a press agent is supposed to begin work on a production approximately four weeks before an Off-Broadway opening and five weeks before a Broadway opening, and they remain with the show for the entire production.

Ideally a press agent should have a year to work on a production, not on a full, structured salary, but with some kind of fee arrangement. This way the producers can take advantage of certain opportunities in terms of coordinating marketing and promotions. This is something that movies do very well, and that the theatre has yet to fully grasp.

After a producer brings his project to a press agent, the agent begins outlining a campaign. He should read the script, and listen to a tape if it's a musical, so that he can come up with ideas for promotion and marketing, find the best advertising agency for the show and create a plan for selling the show to the public.

There are some nitty-gritty basics to the press agent's job: supervising a photo call, putting together a playbill, sending out releases announcing the show. Invitations are sent to the media. Talent interviews are coordinated. An electronic media kit, if the budget warrants it, is put together, and efforts with the marketing and advertising team are coordinated.

If a producer is doing a showcase and looking for a press representative to secure critical coverage, the odds are great that the press rep will not be able to gain the critical coverage desired. There is an opening practically every night of the week. So the likelihood of a showcase being covered is small, unless the show has somebody like Robert DeNiro in the cast. Then press would come, but Robert DeNiro wouldn't want coverage. That's another conundrum the producer could face.

League of Resident Theaters
1501 Broadway, #2401; New York, NY 10036-5503
(212) 944-1501; 768-0785 FAX
Harry H. Weintraub, General Counsel

LORT is a national association of approximately 66 not-for-profit professional theatres which maintains agreements with Actors' Equity Association (AEA), Society of Stage Directors and Choreographers (SSDC), United Scenic Artists (USA); holds semi-annual meetings; is active in collective bargaining and concerns itself with the artistic and management needs of its members.

Lower Manhattan Cultural Council
5 World Trade Center, Suite 9235; New York, NY 10048-0202
(212) 432-0900; 432-3646 FAX
Jenny Dixon, Executive Director

LMCC is an innovative and creative not-for-profit arts service organization which promotes, develops and nurtures New York City downtown cultural resources. LMCC's programs and services include exhibitions and festivals of contemporary art; cultural maps and monthly newsletters about the 165 arts groups under its aegis; grant-giving programs for individual artists; information booths and educational programs for all ages. LMCC produces the Buskars Fare, an annual international festival of street performers, and presents the Women in Jazz concert series. Recently, LMCC, in partnership with a committee of artists and not-for-profit arts organizations, developed Thundergulch, a new laboratory space in Lower Manhattan's Silicon Alley to provide new forms of interaction between artists, audiences and new technologies. LMCC is also the fiscal sponsor and founding member of ABACA, a consortium of SoHo-based visual arts organizations including Art in General, Artists Space, The Drawing Center and Thread Waxing Space.

National Alliance for Musical Theatre
330 West 45th St, Lobby B; New York, NY 10036-3854
(212) 265-5376; 582-8730 FAX
E-mail: NAMTheatre@aol.com
Web: http://www.bway.net/namt
Helen Sneed, Executive Director

When producing new musicals NAMT can be a resource for set and costume rentals, shared physical resources and management and information services. (See Chapter 5: Service Organizations.)

LONG-TERM STRATEGIES MAKE THE NEW GROUP
CLAUDIA CATANIA, EXECUTIVE PRODUCER
THE NEW GROUP, NEW YORK CITY

There is no blueprint for starting one's own theatre. Each endeavor has its own genesis and some wear longer than others. I've been with The New Group since early 1994. In 1991, Scott Elliott formed the group with artists who had studied together and wanted to create work for themselves. A group of this kind is particularly valuable for young directors because they can cut their teeth without the glare of high expectations, and they can work a lot by developing, defining and refining their ideas.

It's important to start small in order to produce repeatedly without breaking the bank. Scott's first partner already had a little space with forty seats. When your friends come to see your show, their twelve dollars should help underwrite the play.

Little by little, admirers make modest offers. One of our first board members contributed by loaning the use of her company's gargantuan Xerox machine. Everybody chipped in some money, time and talent, and the group kept expenses low. The first show cost about $1,000. Members were made up of writers, directors, actors, production people and a couple of brilliant designers (Zaniz, an interior designer, and Kevin Price, an architectural designer). Everyone slaved around the clock, putting things together.

When I joined Scott, we veered away from an actor-based membership because serving the play's best interest often conflicted with serving the actors' needs. And when new companies are established based on the creative needs of actors, directors and playwrights, there is the danger that the producing skill required for longevity is often absent or undeveloped. I went to a show recently that was spectacular, but there was no one in the audience. People sometimes ignore integral components to theatre, which have to do with audience development, marketing, long-term strategies and press. For example, if you are ready to be reviewed you have to acquire an initial hook to get press there. Like in *Gypsy*: "You've got to have a gimmick."

continued on next page

Long-Term Strategies Make The New Group continued

We mounted an exceptional production before Mike Leigh's *Ecstasy*, but it was clearly the draw of Mike Leigh that got the press to cover a New Group play. Prior to that, the press couldn't be counted on. But, they'd heard of Mike Leigh, and that did it. Members of the press who knew independent film came to our show.

For some companies the initial attention-getting device is a name actor or a name director or the clear, niche-like mission of their theatre. You may decide you want to produce plays from the South, and that specificity (any specificity) makes it easier to market, easier for grants, easier for support. It is hard to articulate a mission when you generally just want to do "good theatre," but you will find as you analyze your choices that an overlying principle will emerge.

It takes years to develop foundation and corporate support. Scott and I produced with zero staff for two-and-a-half years, so who had the time to dedicate to development? We had to raise money inventively. When I met Scott he was doing *Cavedwellers*, written by an Armenian American. So I went down to the Armenian Benevolent Society, and they turned out to be very rich. With *Curtains*, which depicted a mercy killing of sorts, the Alzheimer Society did a whole big promotion for us. The most productive way to market is to focus your efforts based on the topic and appeal of your play, on a play-by-play basis. It is easy to identify potential appeal to a particular target audience and it's a great way to broaden your audience base. You can also schedule your choice based on your play's topic. When we considered *My Night with Reg*, a play about six gay men, we just happened to have a slot in June—so we thought, "What a great time to do it, because it's Gay Pride Month."

Another basic way to underwrite a company's effort is to develop skills in non-spending. Every dollar begged, stolen, bartered or borrowed is a dollar earned. Find out how *you* can help that merchant whose product you need. Will a free ad, free tickets, referred customers or a clear and compelling argument help you reduce or eliminate your cost?

As for building a company's momentum, I don't think time matters. For us it was almost a year between *Ecstasy* and *Curtains*. People remember good work. It certainly would be unproductive to put something up that's not your best effort.

National Center for Nonprofit Boards
2000 L St NW, Suite 510; Washington, DC 20036-4907
(202) 452-6262; 452-6299 FAX
E-mail: ncnb@ncnb.org
Web: http://www.ncnb.org
Judith O'Connor, President

The Center seeks to improve the effectiveness and strengthen the leadership of not-for-profit organizations. Services include a board development consultation service and board information center. NCNB also publishes numerous titles on governance, and conducts regional workshops and an annual national meeting.

New York Public Library for the Performing Arts
521 West 43rd St; New York, NY 10036
(212) 870-1643; 496-5196 FAX
E-mail: rmarx@nypl.org
Web: http://www.nypl.org/research/lpa/lpa.html
Robert Marx, Executive Director
and
Theatre Collection Reference Information
(212) 870-1639; 787-3852 FAX
E-mail: rtaylor@nypl.org
Bob Taylor, Curator, Billy Rose Theatre Collection
and
Theatre on Film and Tape Archive
(212) 870-1641; 870-1769 FAX
E-mail: bcorwin@nypl.org
Betty L. Corwin, Project Director

Of particular interest to those producing their own work are the research collections and arts administration books and periodicals in the main collection. References pertaining to other similar theatres give the new producer details of experiences to learn from in forming and running a theatre company. The arts administration books give practical information on finance, administration, marketing, fundraising and other pertinent issues. (See Chapter 5: Service Organizations.)

San Diego Performing Arts League
701 B. St, Suite 225; San Diego, CA 92101-8101
(619) 238-0700; 238-0710 FAX
E-mail: sdpal@cts.com
Web: http://www.sandiego-online.com/sdpal
Alan Ziter, Executive Director

The League advocates, promotes and markets professional performing arts in San Diego County through a variety of programs, including the Times Arts Tix half-price ticket booth, $5 sneak previews, Family Theatre Days, the bimonthly *Performing Arts Guide*, Business Volunteers for the Arts and an annual "pay what you can" Bargain Arts Day.

Small Business Administration
26 Federal Plaza, Room 3100; New York, NY 10278
(212) 264-4354; 264-4963 FAX
Counselor at SCORE

SBA offers services for potential entrepreneurs, including a Start-Up Kit of information on government regulations at the state and federal levels; guidelines for preparing a business plan; and information on small business resources located throughout the New York district that provide training, counseling, loan packaging and publications. SBA also offers loan guaranty programs and management assistance programs, such as Service Corps of Retired Executives (SCORE) and Small Business Development Centers: programs that provide training classes and free management consulting to business owners and would-be entrepreneurs.

Theatre Bay Area
657 Mission St, Suite 402; San Francisco, CA 94105
(415) 957-1557; 957-1556 FAX
E-mail: tba@well.com
Web: http://www.theatrebayarea.org/
Sabrina Klein, Executive Director

A multi-resource communications organization for San Francisco Bay Area theatre workers and companies, TBA owns and operates TIX Bay Area, a full–and half-price ticket booth in downtown San Francisco, and publishes the monthly magazine *Callboard*, the biennial *Theatre Directory of the Bay Area* and other publications. TBA also offers workshops, conferences, general auditions, cooperative advertising, referrals, health insurance, credit-union plans and a discount tickets-by-mail program.

VOLUNTEER LAWYERS FOR THE ARTS
W. E. SCOTT HOOT, ESQ.
NEW YORK CITY

Volunteer Lawyers for the Arts represents artists and arts organizations not otherwise able to afford legal representation. "Artist" is broadly defined by VLA: it includes visual artists, musicians, film makers, writers and performers. VLA handles legal issues for individuals if they're arts related, and any legal issue for an arts-related, not-for-profit organization.

People should think long and hard about the type of entity they form to carry out their project. A lot of decisions made at the beginning of the process, will have to be lived with for a long time. Anyone approaching VLA, who is thinking about incorporating as a not-for-profit arts organization, is required to go through a two-hour seminar designed to help people understand the care and feeding that's required to maintain a not-for-profit corporation on an ongoing basis.

Generally, if you're getting started and you're thinking about what form to take, there are often good reasons not to form a not-for-profit corporation. If, for example, you are undertaking a project that is a one-time deal or has a finite time period to it, there's absolutely no reason to go out and form your own corporation. There are lots of not-for-profit organizations out there under whose umbrella you can do your project. If you want to make a profit, if you personally hope to gain from your enterprise, don't become a not-for-profit corporation. By definition, if you're not-for-profit, any funds that you raise from putting on a production have to be put back into the corporation and used for its charitable purposes. You can pay people reasonable salaries, but you can't at the end of the year say, "Wow, we had a great year let's split the profits."

If you are a control freak, and this is your baby, do not create a corporation, because by law there have to be at least three directors of a corporation. In fact, it's a good idea to have more than three directors if you're an ongoing successful enterprise. And there's a wide variety of people that you should have on your board (fundraisers, program people, an accountant, a lawyer, etc.).

continued on next page

VOLUNTEER LAWYERS FOR THE ARTS CONTINUED

If you are afraid of paperwork, don't become a corporation. Obviously one person that everybody should think about getting on a board is an accountant, because if you do become successful, not only do you have your end-of-year filings with the federal and state governments, but as a not-for-profit organization you will also have employment tax filings, workman's comp filings and unemployment insurance filings, etc. A good accountant on a board makes a lot of sense.

Why would you form a not-for-profit? A lot of people do so because they need other people's money, and the only way to get money from grant-making organizations and individuals is to be a 501(c)(3) charitable entity, to which contributions are tax deductible.

Another good reason to form a corporation is liability. If you're just a bunch of friends putting on a show and there are some legal problems and somebody sues you, you are all personally liable. Once you form a corporation, you protect your personal assets and only the assets of the corporation are at risk.

For organizations that don't have much of a track record, we often suggest that they operate under an umbrella—a fiscal sponsorship—for a year or two. You go to an organization that already has 501(c)(3) status and you operate as a project of that organization. If you don't have an identity, it's also somewhat helpful to be fundraising under the aegis of an umbrella already in existence, that has a track record, and that people know and trust.

Theatre Communications Group (TCG)
355 Lexington Ave; New York, NY 10017
(212) 697-5230; 983-4847 FAX
E-mail: tcg@tcg.org
Web: http://www.tcg.org
Ben Cameron, Executive Director

Not-for-profit theatres which join TCG can take advantage of Finance and Management Services and become part of a national organization which allows for networking with peers at meetings and national conferences. (See Chapter 4: Grants, Fellowships; Chapter 5: Service Organizations.)

THE GENERAL MANAGER
MARSHALL B. PURDY, ASSOCIATE PRODUCER
WALT DISNEY THEATRICALS, NEW YORK CITY

What does a general manager do? He develops a budget, which includes the cost to rehearse and mount the show; build the set, costumes and scenery; and do the initial advertising. I structure my budgets up through the first performance, which is in most cases the first preview.

The general manager also prepares a weekly operating budget, which is the cost of presenting the show on a weekly basis—week in and week out. The two budgets overlap each other in the area of contingency, or in the production budget. You can anticipate that during previews, you will more than likely lose money—your weekly box office receipts are not going to cover your weekly expenses. You need to have cash on hand to cover that short-fall. I try and come up with a reasonable figure, given the project, anticipating what the losses might be during previews.

I do the same thing for the period just after the official opening, because nowadays you can hit a grand slam—you can have a terrific cast and get a great review in the *New York Times*—and the ball really won't start rolling full steam for four, five, six weeks. So again, you have another cash reserve contingency figure that gets plugged into the production budget.

The general manager's second responsibility, once the budgets have been agreed upon, is to start negotiating contracts for directors, designers, actors and any other key personnel. This has to be done within the framework of the budget, as to what you think you can afford, while at the same time fairly paying your talent.

The third area in which the general manager gets involved (in collaboration with a press agent or advertising agency—and if it's a big Broadway show, perhaps with a marketing consultant or an in-house group salesperson) is strategizing what the advertising and marketing plan is going to be. That area has become very important over the last several years.

Theatre Development Fund
1501 Broadway, Suite 2110; New York, NY 10036
(212) 221-0885; 768-1563 FAX
Web: http://www.tdf.org
Jack Goldstein, Executive Director

TDF supports commercial and not-for-profit theatres by providing financial assistance and underwriting ticket sales to selected productions; operating Theatre Centres/TKTS, which markets unsold Broadway and Off-Broadway tickets at a discount on performance day; administering a voucher program for the performing arts; and operating the Costume Collection, a national rental service for not-for-profit organizations. TDF's Theatre Access Project makes theatre accessible to people with disabilities, and their Arts Education programs train and bring thousands of high school students to the theatre. TDF also maintains a 24-hour telephone information service on New York City performing arts events: (212) 768-1818.

Theatre LA
644 South Figueroa St; Los Angeles, CA 90017
(213) 614-0556; 614-0561 FAX
E-mail: theatrela1@aol.com
Web: http://theatrela.org
Alisa Fishbach, Executive Director

Theatre LA is a not-for-profit association of more than 140 theatres and producers throughout greater Los Angeles. It works to unite, represent and promote the theatre community through cooperative marketing programs; the Ovation Awards; their publications, *Theatre LA News* and *Opening Night Calendar*; a theatre management library; workshops; ticketing services; a job bank; an internship program; and through consulting, advice and referral services.

Volunteer Lawyers for the Arts
1 East 53rd St, 6th Floor; New York, NY 10022
(212) 391-2787, 319-2910 (Art Law Line); 752-6575 FAX
E-mail: vlany@bway.net
Amy Schwartzman, Executive Director

VLA provides free legal representation and counseling to eligible artists and not-for-profit arts organizations that have arts-related legal problems. Other services include arts advocacy, and the dissemination of information through publications, legal clinics, workshops and conferences. For information on similar organizations in other cities call the Art Law Line.

CHAPTER 9

WORKING ABROAD AND FOREIGN FESTIVALS

Working abroad can range from taking a production created in the United States to a foreign festival, to fully integrating into another culture, speaking the language of that culture, to producing work with, for instance, resident actors in a repertory theatre in China.

In this chapter you will find information on organizations invaluable to a director or choreographer traveling abroad. Organizations include Arts International (AI) Program, the International Theatre Institute of the United States (ITI/US) and the United States Information Agency (USIA). Martha Coigney, Executive Director of ITI/US, Michèle Assaf, director/choreographer and Christopher Martin, director/designer, give practical advice and personal stories about working abroad. This chapter includes foreign festivals, presented in alphabetical order by country. Each listing contains address information, the type work presented and the period or frequency of the festival. The festival is annual unless otherwise noted.

Several publications that will guide you in your search for working abroad are: Across the Street Around the World: A Handbook for Cultural Exchange by Jennifer Williams; Cultural Organizations in Southeast Asia by Jennifer Lindsay; Guide to Funding for International and Foreign Programs edited by The Foundation Center; Money for International Exchange in the Arts, A Comprehensive Resource Guide edited by ACA Books; Music, Opera, Dance and Drama in Asia, the Pacific and North America (MOD) edited by Arts Publishing International Ltd.; and Performing Arts Year Book for Europe (PAYE) 1996 edited by Arts Publishing International Ltd. For complete information about these books, see Chapter 3: Books and Periodicals.

ORGANIZATIONS

Arts International (AI) Program
Institute of International Education (IIE)
809 United Nations Plaza; New York, NY 10017
(212) 984-5370; 984-5574 FAX
E-mail: ainternational@iie.org
Web: http://www.iie.org/ai
Susan Giordano, Associate Director

Arts International is a division of the Institute of International Education, one of the largest and most active international education and cultural exchange organizations in the U.S. AI encourages relationships between U.S. artists and artists around the world through programs of grants, advocacy, exchange and information. Providing support for the individual artist to live, work and travel in the world is a central goal of AI.

INROADS, an international performing arts initiative developed by Arts International, deepens contact between the U.S. performing arts community and artists in Africa and the Middle East, Latin America and the Caribbean, and Asia and the Pacific Islands. It also increases awareness and understanding among U.S. audiences of the arts of these regions of the world. Grants from INROADS support multidisciplinary and collaborative planning residencies in the U.S. for artists from the above-mentioned regions, working with U.S.-based artists under the umbrella of a U.S. host organization. INROADS has given grants up to $30,000, and offered technical assistance to U.S. not-for-profit dance, theatre, musical theatre, opera, presenting organizations and cultural centers committed to the exploration and development of trans-national projects. Organizations can apply as a single organization or as a consortium. INROADS application deadline is in Apr. For guidelines and more information contact AI.

International Theatre Institute of the United States (ITI/US)
47 Great Jones St; New York, NY 10012
(212) 254-4141; 254-6814 FAX
E-mail: info@iti-usa.org
Web: http://www.iti-usa.org
Martha Coigney, Executive Director

ITI/US's worldwide presence consists of 89 centers on 5 continents. Its main functions are introducing colleagues to theatre life in a given country, coming to the aid of a theatre artist in the case of mistreatment, consulting and advising on international exchange initiatives and matchmaking theatres and artists. Each year more than 100 Americans leave the country armed with ITI/US letters of introduction, I.D. cards, names and schedules.

Some services offered by ITI/US which cater to Americans working abroad are a consulting service, library/information services and theatre exchanges. The consulting service can answer questions about visas, festivals, author's rights, union rules, etc. The library houses more than 6,261 volumes of books, 12,749 programs, 12,733 playscripts and 250 periodicals from 97 countries.

With funding from the United States Information Agency (USIA) and private sources, ITI/US has facilitated directors' and choreographers' work in Argentina, Brazil, Bulgaria, Chile, France, Hungary, Korea, Mexico, Nigeria, Poland, Russia, Turkey, Yugoslavia and Zambia.

United States Information Agency (USIA)
Bureau of Educational and Cultural Affairs; Office of Arts America
301 4th St SW; Washington, DC 20547
(202) 619-4779; 619-6315 FAX
E-mail: jjohnse@usia.gov
Web: http://www.usia.gov/education/arts/pages/index_d.htm

Arts America a division of USIA, administers programming and some funding for individuals and not-for-profit organizations. The projects developed by Arts America are in response to requests from U.S. embassies abroad. The main function of Arts America is to support privately funded artistic ventures abroad by contributing programming, information, referrals and contacts. Arts America has several programs, four of which apply to directors or choreographers: Speakers and Cultural Specialists, Performing Arts, Arts Exchanges, Festivals.

HINTS ABOUT WORKING ABROAD
MARTHA COIGNEY, EXECUTIVE DIRECTOR
INTERNATIONAL THEATRE INSTITUTE OF THE UNITED STATES, NEW YORK CITY

Working abroad, anywhere out of the country, can be a thrilling and life-changing experience, or it can be the pits.

Almost all major problems can be solved by the proper exchange of information—information about where you will be working, information about the company you will work with, information about pay (if there is any), and information about the theatre culture you will be meeting.

Generally, there are three reasons why an otherwise sane and balanced American theatre director or choreographer goes to work "out there." First, an invitation might be given because a director's work is seen abroad at a festival or at a foreign theatre. Second, a director's work is perhaps seen in this country, either at his/her home theatre, or in a theatre where the director has been employed. In this case, the foreign producer, designer, playwright, artistic director might say, "Come on over and do *Three Tall Women* at my theatre next February..." The third, and most frequent, reason would be the urge to "go do it elsewhere."

The following hints apply in all three situations, but they are especially relevant to the director who wants to work in a different place for the first time.

1. Make sure you really want to work abroad.
2. Try to know at least some of the language of the country (even if you think it's English).
3. Learn about the theatre culture of the place you will work. Assume you know nothing!
4. Be as honest as you can with yourself about the level of your experience and the strength of your talent—mistakes in this regard can be very painful far away from home.
5. Take the same care with business arrangements (travel, per diem and other expenses) that you would in the United States.
6. Without an invitation to work in a country, a director must be ready to invest time, some money and lots of care to learn how a theatre

continued on next page

HINTS ABOUT WORKING ABROAD CONTINUED

functions in another place, and how people are introduced into the working community.

7. Ask *everyone* about their experiences directing abroad. No experience is the same, and one person's disaster could be another person's miracle.

8. Before you venture abroad, try your very best to meet with foreign theatre people visiting here. Welcome visiting foreigners here and get to know their work while you can. Try and develop contacts before you leave.

9. Come and see the International Theatre Institute before you go anywhere. ITI/US can provide you with an I.D. card and a letter of introduction (with intent) to theatres in other countries. ITI/US is *not* a job placement service, it is a resource center. We can tell you where good theatres are, in other countries, and how they're organized.

10. Find out from Society of Stage Directors and Choreographers whether any directors from "your country" are available to talk to.

11. If you insist on this perilous adventure, go with joy, patience and the capacity to learn a lot.

FOREIGN FESTIVALS

AUSTRALIA

Adelaide Festival
G.P.O. Box 1269; Adelaide, SA 5001
(011) 61-8-8226-8111; 61-8-8226-8100 FAX
E-mail: ausfest@adelaide.on.net
Web: http://www.festivals.on.net
Robyn Archer, Artistic Director

Presents: Modern ballet, modern dance, classical ballet, theatre. **Period/Frequency:** Feb–Mar (biennial).

Melbourne International Festival of the Arts (MIFA)
Box 7550; Melbourne, VIC 3004
(011) 61-3-9866-8866; 61-3-9820-3611 FAX
Clifford Hocking, Artistic Director

Presents: Multimedia, musical theatre **Period/Frequency:** Oct or Nov.

BELGIUM

Fondation Europalia International—Biennale des Arts et de la Culture
10 Rue de Royale; 1000 Brussels
(011) 32-2-507-8550; 32-2-513-5488 FAX
Madou Moulaert, Theatre and Dance Director

Presents: Theatre, dance. **Period/Frequency:** Sept–Dec.

International Kunsten FESTIVAL des Arts—Brussels
Brussels International Arts Festival; Quai du Commerce 18; 1000 Brussels
(011) 32-2-219-0707; 32-2-218-7453 FAX
Frie Leysen and Guido Minne, Artistic Directors

Presents: Dance, theatre. **Period/Frequency:** May (biennial).

BULGARIA

Varna Summer International Theatre Festival
43 8th Primorski Polk St; 9000 Varna
(011) 359-52-220-101, 359-52-222-425; 359-52-253-011 FAX
Mincho Minchev, Artistic Manager

Presents: Theatre. **Period/Frequency:** Jun.

CANADA

British Columbia Festival of the Arts
300-764 Yates St; Victoria, BC V8W 1L4
604-920-4118; 356-0092 FAX
Gabrielle Levin, Artistic Director

Presents: Modern dance, classical ballet, classical theatre. **Period/Frequency:** May.

EXPERIENCE ANOTHER CULTURE
MICHÈLE ASSAF, DIRECTOR, CHOREOGRAPHER, TEACHER
NEW YORK CITY/LOS ANGELES

Many foreign countries want the American culture, in art and mind. However, be prepared not to live an American lifestyle while abroad. Your hosts want you to experience their culture. Here's some advice to those who venture abroad.

1. If you work abroad, make sure you have a paid, round-trip ticket in hand before you go.
2. Insist on getting paid your fee, in your own currency. You will almost always lose money if you have to exchange it. Get it wired ahead of time, if you can, so you avoid hassle and the chance of delayed payment once you're there.
3. You will build a reputation if you are easy to get along with and do good work. You must show an appreciation for the foreign country you are visiting, and respect their way of doing things, such as rehearsal and tech scheduling. It's different in every country. You're not in America!
4. Your colleagues appreciate when you try to speak their language.
5. Always have a translator. Make sure that he/she is someone who knows the theatre, like the assistant director. If you make the mistake of getting a translator who has no knowledge of theatre, he/she will translate everything you say literally, word-for-word, instead of expressing the emotion or idea you are trying to convey.
6. It's a nice gesture to bring American gifts. It's always appreciated. The gifts don't need to be expensive, though there are times when expensive gifts are appropriate, like for a particularly important producer.
7. Enjoy the experience! It might never happen again.

Carrefour International de Théâtre
Carrefour International de Théâtre de Quebec; 156 Rue St. Paul, Bureau 101;
C.P. 518, succ. Haute-Ville; Quebec City, PQ G1R 4R8
418-692-3131; 692-5638 FAX
Michel Bernatchez and Pierre MacDuff, Artistic Directors

Presents: Contemporary theatre, theatre in repertoire, theatre for young audiences. **Period/Frequency:** May (biennial).

Festival de Théâtre des Amériques/Theatre Festival of the Americas
C.P. 507, Succ. Desjardins; Montreal, PQ H5B 1B6
514-842-0704; 842-3795 FAX
Marie-Hélène Falcon, General and Artistic Director

Presents: Modern theatre, classical theatre, innovative theatre. **Period/Frequency:** May–Jun.

Shaw Festival Theatre Foundation
Box 774; Niagara-on-the-Lake, ON L0S 1J0
905-468-2153; 468-5438 FAX
E-mail: publicitydept.:publicty@shawfest.com
Web: http://www.shawfest.com/shaw.html
Christopher Newton, Artistic Director

Presents: Classical theatre from 1856–1950. **Period/Frequency:** Apr–Oct.

Stratford Festival
Box 520; Stratford, ON N5A 6V2
519-271-4040; 271-2734 FAX
Web: http://www.ffa.ucalgary.ca/stratford/
Richard Monette, Artistic Director

Presents: Musical theatre, classical theatre, modern theatre. **Period/Frequency:** May–Oct.

Vancouver International Children's Festival
601 Cambie St, Suite 301;Vancouver, BC V6B 2P1
604-687-7697; 669-3613 FAX
E-mail: kidsfest@youngarts.ca
Web: http://www.wimsey.com/youngarts
Marjorie Maclean, Executive Director

Presents: Musical theatre, operetta, multimedia, opera, modern ballet, modern dance, modern theatre, classical theatre. **Period/Frequency:** May–Jun.

CHINA

Hong Kong Arts Festival
(See Hong Kong, page 194.)

CROATIA

Dubrovnik Festival
Dubrovacki Wetnji Festival Dubrovnik; 20000 Dubrovnik
(011) 385-20-412-288; 385-20-27944 FAX
Dubravka Knezevic, Director

Presents: Drama, opera, dance, folklore. **Period/Frequency:** Jul–Aug.

CUBA

Festival de Teatro de la Habana
Calle 4 #257 e/ 11 y 13 Plaza; 10400 Vedado Habana 4
(011) 53-7-304-351; 53-7-333-610-810 FAX
Elberto Garcia, Director

Presents: Folk dance, modern ballet, modern dance, classical theatre. **Period/Frequency:** Sept–Oct (biennial; next festival 2000).

CYPRUS

Kypria International Festival
Ministry of Education & Culture; 20 Byron's Ave.; Nicosia
(011) 357-2-302-442, 303-337; 357-2-443-565 FAX
George Moleskis and Marina Economou-Stavrinidi, Cultural Officers

Presents: Theatre, dance, opera. **Period/Frequency:** Sept.

MAKING CONTACTS ABROAD
CHRISTOPHER MARTIN, DIRECTOR, DESIGNER, COMPOSER
NEW YORK CITY

In 1979, I began to spend more and more time abroad, eager to unlock the great mystery of the European repertory system. In particular, I was attracted by the work of Roger Planchon and the Théâtre National Populaire in Lyon, and that of Peter Stein and the Schaubühne am Halleschen Ufer in West Berlin. After introducing myself, and explaining my interest in their work, both companies opened their doors to me, and I spent as much time in rehearsal and behind the scenes as I desired. I was able to lay the path for working abroad in the future.

At that time, directors were highly respected as dedicated artists, and actors were often engaged for lifetime contracts. These days, things are changing, and the situation abroad is being governed by economics, as it is in the U.S. The great directors no longer head companies, actors choose to work freelance, and with spiraling ticket prices and failing attendance, theatres look more and more toward the Broadway musical to save the day. But despite this, working abroad can still be a worthwhile experience for an artist.

Advice for those wishing to work abroad:

1. Make contacts. In person. People give opportunities to people, not to résumés.
2. Become acquainted with the International Theatre Institute (ITI/US)—the UNESCO organization set up to foster global communication between theatre professionals. ITI/US has offices in every major country, and can prove indispensable in finding your way into each theatre system, learning what you should see and whom to meet.
3. English is the universal language, and most theatre pros can speak enough to communicate with you. But, be wary of using too much slang (most Europeans know British English). Speak slowly and clearly. Knowing some French, German or Russian (if you are in Eastern Europe) is a great help—although English is fast taking over.
4. You need to know the basics of a country's vocabulary so you can

continued on next page

decipher playing schedules and repertoire, and to purchase tickets not arranged by ITI/US. And, know as much as you can of the culture and work habits of the people you visit, so you don't step on anyone's toes.

5. If you secure work, insist on *two* assistants/interpreters. You'll need one to translate for you, the other to act as a production stage manager. The job of stage manager, as we know it, simply does not exist. In all my travels, the only place (other than Great Britain) where I found stage managers was in South Korea. Every person on the tech and production staff is his own boss, and things get done by miracle, not by organization.

6. Foreign actors rehearse only four hours a day, usually in the morning. It is sometimes possible to get an additional three hours in the evening, but only if the actors are not engaged in performance. Also, theatres often engage guest actors who are frequently unavailable even for day rehearsal due to commitments in other cities. You need to plan your time carefully.

7. Get to know the tech crew. Make them your friends. Otherwise, you're dead. To most of them, it's a time-punch job. Show them that you care about them, and the miracles you need will happen.

8. Be wary of management. Once you've begun rehearsals, they tend to forget your project and concentrate on the next. You'll be left to fend for yourself.

9. Long-standing permanent companies can be deadly. No one can be fired or disciplined except in extreme cases (drunk on the job, taking a TV gig without prior clearance). Often, they take company time to deal with personal things like the dentist. Get them to love you, and you'll begin to shake the dust off the system.

10. Unless you find yourself in a capital city like Paris or Berlin, there is little to do with your free time. The theatre folk head home to their families, and the cities shut down early. If you are not rehearsing in the evening, you'll need a good deal of reading matter or future work, otherwise you're stuck with foreign language TV and a lonely hotel room.

11. Learn to play the game, and you'll have a great time. The experience will be well worth whatever trouble you have in getting to opening night. You'll make friends for life.

DENMARK

The Aarhus Festival
Officersbygningen; Vester Allé 3; 8000 Aarhus C
(011) 45-8931-8270, 45-8931-8272; 45-8619-1336 FAX
Lars Seeberg, Artistic Director

Presents: Opera, ballet, modern dance, theatre. **Period/Frequency:** Sept.

FINLAND

Helsinki Festival
Helsingin Juhlaviikot; Rauhankatu 7E; 00170 Helsinki
(011) 358-9-135-4522; 358-9-278-1578 FAX
Web: http://www.hel.fi or www.hartwall.fi
Web: http://www.kaapeli.fi/~kirja/lp/
Risto Nieminen, Director

Presents: Dance, theatre. **Period/Frequency:** Aug.

Savonlinna Opera Festival
Savolinnan Oopperajuhlat; Olavinkatu 27; 57130 Savolinna
(011) 358-15-576-750; 358-15-531-866 FAX
Jorma Hynninen, Artistic Director

Presents: Opera. **Period/Frequency:** Jul.

Tampere International Theatre Festival
Tampereen Teatterikesä; Tullikamarinaukio 2; 23100 Tampere
(011) 358-3-214-0992; 358-2-223-0121 FAX
Otso Kautto, Artistic Director

Presents: Theatre, comedy, dance theatre. **Period/Frequency:** Aug.

FRANCE

Festival d'Automne
156 rue de Rivoli; 75001 Paris
(011) 33-1-4296-1227; 33-1-4015-9288 FAX
Alain Crombecque, General Director

Presents: Contemporary dance, modern theatre. **Period/Frequency:** Sept–Dec.

Festival d'Avignon
8 bis rue de Mons; 84000 Avignon
(011) 33-4-9027-6650; 33-4-9027-6683 FAX
Bernard Faivre d'Arcier, Director

Presents: Theatre, contemporary dance. **Period/Frequency:** Jul.

Festival International des Francophonies en Limousin
11 Ave. du Général de Gaulle; 87000 Limoges
(011) 33-5-5510-9010; 33-5-5577-0472 FAX
Monique Blin, Director

Presents: Contemporary theatre. **Period/Frequency:** Sept–Oct.

GERMANY

Berliner Festwochen
Berliner Festspiele; Budapester Straße 50; 10787 Berlin
(011) 49-0-30-254-890
Ulrich Eckhardt, Director

Presents: Theatre. **Period/Frequency:** Sept.

Bonner Biennale
Schauspiel Bonn; Am Michaelshof 9; D 53177 Bonn
(011) 49-228-820-8253, 49-228-820-8254;
49-228-820-8133 FAX
Web: http://www.psychologie.uni-bonn.de/sonstige/theater/bien_98/biennale_r.htm
Manfred Beilharz, Tankred Dorst and Iris Laufenberg, Directors

Presents: New European drama. **Period/Frequency:** Jun (biennial).

Tanz und Theater International
c/o Tanz und Theaterbüro Hannover; Roscherstr, 12; 30161 Hannover
(011) 49-511-343-919; 49-511-331-965
Christiane Winter, Festival Director

Presents: Dance, theatre. **Period/Frequency:** Sept.

Theatre of the World
Theater der Welt; Schloßstr. 48; 12165 Berlin
(011) 49-30-791-1692; 49-30-791-1874 FAX
E-mail: itigermany@aol.com
Web: http://www.users.aol.com/itigermany/welcome.htm
Martin Roeder Zerndt, Director

Presents: International theatre. **Period/Frequency:** Jun-Jul (country roving triennial). For more information contact Mr. Roeder Zerndt at the German International Theatre Institute (011) 49-30-791-1777.

Theatretreffen Berlin
Berliner Festspiele; Budapester Strasse 50; 10787 Berlin
(011) 49-30-254-890; 49-30-2548-9111
Ulrich Eckhardt, Director

Presents: Theatre for German-speaking countries. **Period/Frequency:** May.

GREECE

Epidaurus Festival
Greek Tourism Organisation; Voukourestiou 1; 10564 Athens
(011) 30-1-323-1291; 30-1-323-5172, 30-1-753-2208 FAX
Nikoforos Giegos, Director

Presents: Classical Greek and Latin drama. **Period/Frequency:** Jun–Aug.

HONG KONG

Hong Kong Arts Festival
13/F Hong Kong Arts Centre; 2 Harbour Rd; Wanchai, Hong Kong
(011) 852-2824-3555; 852-2824-3798, 852-2824-3722 FAX
Kau Ng, Executive Director

Presents: Opera, musical theatre, classical theatre, modern theatre. **Period/Frequency:** Jan–Feb.

HUNGARY

Internationale Meeting of Moving Theatres
Nemzetközi Mozgasszinházi Talalkóz; Szkéné Theatre;
Muegyetem Rakpart 3; 1111 Budapest
(011) 36-1-463-2451; 36-1-463-2450 FAX
János Regos and Pál Regos, Directors

Presents: Moving theatre. **Period/Frequency:** Oct.

ISRAEL

The Israel Festival
Box 4409; Jerusalem 91044
(011) 972-2-561-1438; 972-2-566-9850 FAX
Micah Lewensohn, Artistic Director

Presents: Dance, theatre. **Period/Frequency:** May–Jun.

ITALY

Festival dei du Mondi (Spoleto)
Associazione Festival dei due Mondi;
Sede Legale: 06049 Spoleto—Piazza Duomo 8
(011) 0743-45028-220320; 0743-45028-220321 FAX
Gian Carlo Menotti, President and Artistic Director

Presents: Opera, ballet, theatre. **Period/Frequency:** Jun–Jul.

Festival Internazionale Inteatro (Polverigi)
Piazzi Cavour 29; 60121 Ancona
(011) 39-0-71-200-442, 39-0-71-205-274;
39-0-71-205-274 FAX
Web: http://www.bancmarche.it/teatro/festival/polverigi/index.htm
Velia Papa, Artistic Director

Presents: Dance, theatre. **Period/Frequency:** Jul.

JAPAN

BeSeTo Theatre Festival
BeSeTo Engekisai; 302, 2-14-19 Shimo-Ochiai; Shinjuku-ku, Tokyo 161
(011) 81-3-3951-5706; 81-3-3951-5806 FAX
Tadashi Suzuki, Co-Director

Presents: Theatre. **Period/Frequency:** Nov.

Kyoto Arts Festival
Geijutsu-Saiten Kyo; 1 Shimogamo Tsukamoto-cho; Sakyo-ku, Kyoto 606
(011) 81-75-723-7719; 81-75-711-5101 FAX
Sumiko Endo, Artistic Director

Presents: International modern theatre, dance. **Period/Frequency:** May.

Toga Festival
Kami-Momose; Toga-mura Higashi-Tonami-gun; Toyama 939-25
(011) 81-763-68-2356; 81-763-68-2912 FAX
Tadashi Suzuki, Artistic Director

Presents: International theatre, dance. **Period/Frequency:** Jul-Aug.

Tokyo International Festival of Performing Arts (TIF)
Tokyo Kokusai Butai Geijutsu Festival; c/o PARC JAPAN;
5B, 7-3-12 Roppongi; Minato-ku, Tokyo 106
(011) 81-3-3423-7574; 81-3-3423-6984 FAX
E-mail: tifpa@ppp.bekkoame.or.jp
Tadao Nakane, Producing Director

Presents: Theatre, dance, opera. **Period/Frequency:** Fall.

REPUBLIC OF KOREA

Seoul Theatre Festival
National Theatre Association of Korea; 4th Floor, Yechong Bldg;
1-117 Dongsoong-dong; Jongro-gu, Seoul 110-510
(011) 82-2-744-8055; 82-2-766-4868 FAX
Jin-soo Jung, Artistic Director

Presents: Theatre. **Period/Frequency:** Aug–Sept.

LITHUANIA

Lithuanian International Theatre Festival (LIFE)
Lietuvos Tarptautinis Teatro Festivalis; J. Basanaviciaus Str. 5; 2683 Vilnius
(011) 370-2-662-668; 370-2-632-930 FAX
Ruta Vanagaite, Executive Director

Presents: Theatre. **Period/Frequency:** Annual.

MACEDONIA

Open Theatre Festival
Mlad Otvoren Teater; Kej Dimitar Vlahov bb; 91000 Skopje
(011) 389-91-115-225; 389-91-115-906 FAX
Ljubisa Nikodinovski, Director

Presents: Experimental, alternative theatre. **Period/Frequency:** Apr–May.

MEXICO

Festival International Cervantino
Alvaro Obregon 273, Col. Roma Norte; 06700 México D.F.
(011) 52-5-207-4764, 52-5-207-4824; 52-5-533-4122 FAX
Julieta Gonzalez, Programming Director

Presents: Multimedia, musical theatre, opera. **Period/Frequency:** Oct.

Festival Internacional de Arte Contemporaneo en León
c/o Consejo para la Cultura de León, Pedro Moreno; 202, 37000 León Gto.
(011) 52-47-164-301; 52-47-140-326 FAX
Ana Maria Riveira, Director

Presents: Multimedia, dance, theatre. **Period/Frequency:** Annual.

MONACO

Printemps des Arts de Monte—Carlo
Direction des Affaires Culturelles; 8 rue Louis Notari; 98000 Monte Carlo
(011) 377-9315-8303; 377-9350-6694 FAX
Rainier Rocchi, Director

Presents: Ballet, opera, theatre. **Period/Frequency:** Apr–May.

NETHERLANDS

Holland Festival
Kleine Gartmanplantsoen 21; 1017 RP Amsterdam
(011) 31-20-627-6566; 31-20-620-3459 FAX
Jan van Vlijmen, Director

Presents: Opera, dance, theatre. **Period/Frequency:** Jun.

NORWAY

Bergen International Festival
Festspillene I Bergen; Box 183; 5001 Bergen
(011) 47-5531-2170; 47-5531-5531 FAX
Bergljót Jónsdóttir, Artistic and Managing Director

Presents: Opera, ballet, theatre. **Period/Frequency:** May–Jun.

Ibsen Stage Festival
Nationaletheatret Stortingsgaten 15; 0161 Oslo 1
(011) 47-2241-1640, 47-2242-4343; 47-2242-4343, 47-420-355 FAX
Ellen Horn, Artistic Director

Presents: Ibsen plays and performances based on Ibsen's work **Period/ Frequency:** Aug–Sept.

POLAND

Warsaw Theatre Meetings
Warszawskie Spotkania Teatralne; Pl Pilusudskiego 9; 00-950 Warszawa
(011) 48-22-635-6352; 48-22-261-849 FAX
Mieczyslaw Marszycki, Director

Presents: Theatre. **Period/Frequency:** Nov–Dec.

ROMANIA

Piatra Neamtz Theatre Festival
1 Stefan cel Mare Square; 5600 Piatra Neamtz
(011) 40-33-611-472; 40-33-617-159 FAX
Nicolae Scarlat, Director

Presents: Theatre. **Period/Frequency:** May.

SINGAPORE

Singapore Festival of Arts
c/o National Arts Council; 460 Alexandra Rd; Singapore 119962
(011) 65-270-0722; 65-273-6882 FAX
Liew Chin Choy, Director

Presents: Theatre, dance. **Period/Frequency:** May–Jun (biennial).

SPAIN

Cadiz Ibero—America Theatre Festival
Festival Iberoamericano de Teatro de Cádiz; Fundación Municipal
de Cultura; c/o Isabel la Católica; Nffl 12; 11004 Cádiz
(011) 34-56-221-680, 34-56-211-123, 34-56-227-624; 34-56-222-051 FAX
José Bablé Neira, Artistic Director

Presents: Theatre, dance. **Period/Frequency:** Oct.

Granada International Theatre Festival
Festival Internacional de Teatro de Granada; Ayuntamiento de Granada–
Concejalio de Cultura; c/o Cuesta de Santa Ines 6; 18010 Granada
(011) 34-58-224-384, 34-58-229-344; 34-58-227-778 FAX
Director

Presents: Avant-garde theatre, dance. **Period/Frequency:** May.

SWEDEN

North…South-ETC Theatre Festival
c/o Stockholm City Theatre; Box 164 12; 103 27 Stockholm
(011) 46-8-700-0100; 46-8-411-8568 FAX
Ferelith Lean, Director

Presents: New theatre. **Period/Frequency:** Sept.

TAIWAN

International Festival of the Arts
c/o Chiang Kai-Shek Cultural Centre; 67 Wu-Fu 1st Rd; Kaohsiung City
(011) 886-7-222-5141, 886-7-222-2911; 886-7-224-8764 FAX
Program Director

Presents: Theatre, dance. **Period/Frequency:** Sept–Nov.

TURKEY

Istanbul International Theatre Festival
Uluslararasi Istanbul Tiyatro Festivali; Istanbul Foundation for Culture
and Arts; Istiklal Cad. Luvr. Ap. No. 146; Beyoglu, Istanbul
(011) 90-212-293-3133, 90-212-293-3134, 90-212-293-3135;
90-212-249-5667 FAX
Melih Fereli, General Director

Presents: Theatre. **Period/Frequency:** May.

UNITED KINGDOM

Edinburgh Festival Fringe
Edinburgh Festival Fringe Society; 180 High St; Edinburgh (Scotland) EH1 1QS
(011) 44-131-226-5257, 44-131-226-5259; 44-131-220-4205 FAX
E-mail: admin@edfringe.org.uk
Web: http://www.presence.co.uk/fringe
Hilary Strong, Director

Presents: All performing arts. **Period/Frequency:** Aug.

Edinburgh International Festival
21 Market St; Edinburgh (Scotland) EH1 1BW
(011) 44-131-226-4001; 44-131-225-1173 FAX
Brian McMaster, Festival Director

Presents: Opera, theatre, dance. **Period/Frequency:** Aug–Sept.

Glasgow-Mayfest
129 High St; Glasgow (Scotland) G1 1PH
(011) 44-141-552-8444; 44-141-552-6612 FAX
E-mail: mayfest@cqm.co.uk
Paul Bassett, Artistic Director

Presents: Dance, theatre, comedy. **Period/Frequency:** May.

London International Festival of Theatre (LIFT)
19–20 Great Sutton St; London EC1V ODN
(011) 44-171-490-3964, 44-171-490-3965; 44-171-490-3976 FAX
E-mail: lift@mail.easynet.co.uk
Web: http://www.openservices.co.uk/lift.html
Rose De Wend Fenton, Artistic Director

Presents: Contemporary theatre. **Period/Frequency:** Jun-Jul (biennial).

Stratford Festival
Stratford Festival Company; Ryon Hill House; Warwick Rd;
Stratford-upon-Avon CV37 ONZ
(011) 44-1789-267-969, 44-1789-294-997; 44-1789-297-471,
44-1789-294-997 FAX
E. J. Beare and Roger Rippin, Trustees

Presents: Theatre. **Period/Frequency:** Jul.

YUGOSLAVIA

BITEF—Belgrade International Theatre Festival
BITEF—Beogradski Interncionalni Teatarski Festival;
Terazije 29/l; 11000 Belgrade
(011) 381-11-335-729, 381-11-332-437, 381-11-343-966;
381-11-687-854 FAX
Jovan Cirilov, Artistic Director

Presents: Avant-garde, experimental theatre. **Period/Frequency:** Sept.

CHAPTER 10

NEW
MEDIA

New technologies are developed every day that may enhance the theatrical experience or lead to a new kind of performance on their own. Director and cyber expert, Stephen A. Schrum, takes you through various possibilities in this chapter, including an introduction to some of the terminology being used, insights into what has been happening with performance in cyberspace, and some ideas of how your skills as a director or choreographer may be utilized in these ventures.

This chapter is divided into five sections: Chats and MOOs, Interactive Web Pages, VRML and Virtual Worlds, MIDI and Video Conferencing. Throughout this volume, we have listed Web Sites for organizations whenever possible. Here we have included additional Web Sites related to theatre, directing and choreography, which may offer useful information or lead you to it.

COMPUTER APPLICATION AND RESOURCES

All Web Site addresses are enclosed within < >; these are not part of the address, and are used only to distinguish Web addresses from this volume's text.

CHATS AND MOOS

Internet Relay Chat (IRC)

IRC is a large text-based chat system that encompasses many networks world-wide. Users connect to it by telnet (a simple network connection program) or by an IRC client (such as IRCle and HOMER), and then communicate with other users around the world. See <http://clients.undernet.org/> for a list of clients.

One of the first uses of online technology for performance occurred on IRC. On 12 December 1993, Stuart Harris directed *HAMNET*, Shakespeare's *Hamlet* adapted for the medium of IRC, and presented on channel #hamnet. The script consisted of seventeen roles (including Ophelia, Hamlet, Enter, Exit, Drums) and eighty lines of dialogue, a kind of online Reduced Shakespeare Company *Hamlet*.

The Journal of Computer-Mediate Communication has more information on *HAMNET*:

Introduction: <http://www.ascusc.org/jcmc/vol1/issue2/intro.html>;
The script: <http://shum.huji.ac.il/jcmc/vol1/issue2/script.html>.

MOOs

When mainframes were first being used by universities, students began writing programs to create virtual environments called MUDs, or Multi-User Dungeons or Dimensions. Although these online universes originally served as sites for many dungeons-and-dragons-type worlds, MUDs, and later MOOs (MUDs with Object-Oriented programming), have been taken over for educational purposes. They are used for online meetings, classes and, now, for performance.

A MOO is a text-based virtual reality, and everything is rendered as text. Dialogue appears like this: "SteveS says 'Hello!'" So-called emotes or actions appear as stage directions: "SteveS jumps up to the ceiling and grabs the chandelier." Because of the text-based nature of MOOs, and because everything utilizes the player's (as users are called) imagination, anything is possible within these virtual worlds.

Formerly, users connected to MOOs via telnet, by inputting the address of a MOO (e.g., purple-crayon.media.mit.edu) and a port number (e.g., 8888) to reach a MOO such as MIT's MediaMOO. Now, however, there are other client programs available. (A client is a computer program that has one particular function.)

Clients for connecting to MOOs include:

Surf and Turf (which works on Web browsers with JAVA) <http://www.bvu.edu/ctown/stclient.html>;

MudDweller (for Macintosh) <http://tecfa.unige.ch/pub/software/mac/Applications/Reseau/muddweller-12.hqx>;

MacMOOSE (for Macintosh) <http://asb.www.media.mit.edu/people/asb/MacMOOSE>;

Pueblo (Windows) <http://www.chaco.com/pueblo/contents.html>;

tinyfugue (for UNIX) <ftp://muds.okstate.edu/pub/jds/clients/UnixClients/>.

Information of other clients can be found through: <http://tecfa.unige.ch/edu-comp/WWW-VL/eduVR-page.html#Clients>.

ATHEMOO

Among the educational MOOs available is ATHEMOO, found at <telnet://moo.hawaii.edu:9999>.

In 1997, several experiments in theatre took place on ATHEMOO: *Net–Seduction*, a play by Stephen A. Schrum; *A Place For Souls*, written by Twyla Mitchell-Shiner; and an interactive environment based on Kafka's book *The Metamorphosis*, entitled, *MetaMOOphosis*, created by Rick Sacks. (The latter is still available for use; see <http://www.io.org/rikscafe/Kafka> for details.)

The basics of MOOing can be found at <http://tecfa.unige.ch/moo/book2/node1.html>.

For more about MOOs for education, contact <http://mbhs.bergtraum.k12.ny.us/moo.html>.

For more background from an academic perspective, go to <http://lucien.sims.berkeley.edu/moo.html>.

For a listing of other available MOOs, see <http://central.itp.berkeley.edu/~thorne/MOO.html>.

While MOOs have been limited to text-only displays, new software is allowing connections between MOOs and Web pages (dubbed WOOs), to add the dimensions of sight and sound. By typing a simple command, a player can cause the spectators' Web browsers to access a particular graphic at a specified time, or can connect to a sound or MIDI (Musical Instrument Digital Interface) file, and thus supply music and sound effects.

For a demonstration, connect to ATHEMOO through your Web browser via <http://moo.hawaii.edu/athemoo/WebMOO.html>.

CREATING THEATRE IN CYBERSPACE
STEPHEN A. SCHRUM, PROFESSOR, THEATRE ARTS
UNIVERSITY OF CHARLESTON, WEST VIRGINIA

For the director looking to expand beyond the world of live theatre, or even film and video, the Internet and World Wide Web are rapidly becoming possible venues in which theatre and dance practitioners can work. In recent years, directors, choreographers, designers and playwrights have begun using computers and the Internet to collaborate and share information in the preproduction process. Soon, with increasing technological developments, the online world will no longer be confined to E-mail and static Web pages, but will become a new environment for performance.

Some critics voice concern that theatre cannot be presented online, because theatre requires interaction between the actor and the audience. While this is true of the current state of the technology (online performance is closer to video and film, and is a one-way communication), upcoming advances in computer hardware and software will allow for greater interactivity between those performing and the spectators for whom they perform.

A few cyberspace pioneers already have begun experimenting in this area. Though some of these computer applications are not always geared for performance, they can be adapted for performance, in the same way that some twentieth century art movements began solely on canvases, and later found their way to the stage.

Of course, creating an online performance adds a new level of possible problems. The performer and/or spectator may encounter lag time (system slowdown), system crashes, hardware breakdowns, Internet disconnections, synchronization problems and software that just doesn't do what you want it to do. However, planning for any contingency, as well as using the limitations created by the technology to your advantage, can provide astounding results. (Think of it as using rehearsal cubes, the actors' abilities and the audience's imagination in a black box space, rather than having the resources to create the Broadway stage setting of Phantom of the Opera.)

Online theatre is in its infancy, but as more people experiment

continued on next page

NEW MEDIA, NEW STAGES, NEW WORLDS CONTINUED

with the technology and push back its boundaries, we will see more and more productions taking place on the Web and Internet. Perhaps by 2020 (the year of perfect vision), we may have the ability to interact one-on-one with actors on a stage from far away, or even with many actors on different stages in different locations in front of a computer-generated setting. Oh, brave new computer-generated world!

Other Chat Forms

The Palace <http://www.palacespace.com/index.html> presents the user with a two-dimensional graphic interface for "live Web-based multimedia communication among multiple users." Their Web Site lists these possible uses: Electronic Commerce, Customer Support, Distance Learning. Palace sites promoting films (such as *Independence Day*), computer games and chatting are available.

In 1997, as part of the Crosswaves Festival, Cat Hebert of the Virtual Drama Society at <http://www.virtualdrama.com/>, arranged for the performance of a short mystery to be performed on a Palace site. Avatars (on-screen representations of the actors) moved about the various rooms, speaking and interacting for the audience.

While no one has begun using other forms of chat for performances as of yet, these online venues do provide the user with a paratheatrical atmosphere filled with role-playing, gender-pretending and, yes, the beginnings of theatre.

WebChat uses Web pages that are set up with JAVA scripts (JAVA being a cross-platform scripting language), simple HTML (hypertext markup language, that gives Web pages their formatting), and other computer scripts. Some of these are available for free, so that you can set up your own chat page. In addition, you can set up a private room on a public chat server and have closed meetings.

Examples of Web-Based Chat

The Gathering Place <http://www.paniczone.com>;
The chat forum page <http://www.paniczone.com/chat/forums.pl>;
The Park <http://www.the-park.com/>;
Webchat Broadcasting System <http://wbs.net/>.

Setting Up a Chat Page

To set up a chat page with Parachat that uses their server, contact <http://www.parachat.com/>.

There is also other chat software available. While not necessarily "theatrical" in their use, they are helpful for quick one-to-one messaging:

PowWow <http://www.tribal.com>;
ICQ <http://www.mirabilis.com>;
PAL (Personal Access List) <http://talk.excite.com/communities/excite/pal/>.

INTERACTIVE WEB PAGES

Many people know that Web pages can deliver content one way (from server to consumer), but they also can be interactive. Besides using a chat function, users can download photos, edit them, and then upload them to the original server for display. While the interactive component is not seamless as of yet, the foundation is there. Users may also submit sound and music files, and become part of a virtual interactive orchestra. It is important to note that one needn't be a tech head to learn these things; a working theatre artist can learn it in a brief time, and there are many online tutorials:

HTML Developer's Jumpstation
<http://oneworld.wa.com/htmldev/devpage/dev-page1.html>;
Intro to HTML <http://www.cwru.edu/help/introHTML/toc.html>;
JAVA tutorial <http://java.sun.com/docs/books/tutorial/>.

VRML AND VIRTUAL WORLDS

Some designers use 3-D computer graphics in the planning and preproduction process, while other theatre artists are beginning to create immersive spaces with hardware and software. Using Virtual Reality Markup Language (VRML), designers can create settings quickly and easily, which can be viewed with Web browsers (Netscape Navigator and Communicator, or Microsoft Internet Explorer), regardless of computer platform (such as Mac or Windows).

One of the first people to use computer projections to surround the audience was George Coates, who in his George Coates Performance Works productions <http://www.georgecoates.org/>, has extended the boundaries of immersive theatre. In early performances, high-end projectors surrounded the audience with quickly changing textures and settings. A later performance, entitled *The Nowhere Band*, featured musicians appearing and playing together on stage through the use of videoconferencing software (see below). Audience members, connected with the same software, could also become part of the show.

Another use of projected scenery occurred in the science fiction music-drama, *1000 Airplanes on the Roof*, a collaboration by Philip Glass, David Henry Hwang and Jerome Sirlin (libretto published by Gibbs-Smith, 1989). While the audience was not surrounded by the projections, the technology demonstrated an effective use of quickly changing scenery mirroring the rapidly changing psychological state of the character.

The work of i.e.VR, the Institute for the Exploration of Virtual Realities <http://kuhttp.cc.ukans.edu/~mreaney/> at the University of Kansas, has been widely publicized <http://kuhttp.cc.ukans.edu/~mreaney/biblio.html>. Beginning with Elmer Rice's *The Adding Machine* in 1995, they have continued experimenting with virtual reality settings in Arthur Kopit's *Wings* (1996) and *Tesla Electric* (1997).

KU grad student, Lance Gharavi, has done additional work in this area with a production of *Samuel Beckett's Play*. About the same time, David Saltz, working at the State University of New York at Stony Brook, helped create BeckettSpace, an interactive theatrical environment. This installation presented eight of Beckett's plays, blending live actors and computer hardware and software. [Stephen A. Schrum's forthcoming book, *Theatre in Cyberspace: Issues of Teaching, Acting and Directing*, contains essays by both on their projects.]

An experiment in April 1998, attempted to produce Shakespeare's *Midsummer Night's Dream* over the Web. According to the informational Web page <http://www.shoc.com/vrmldream/>:

> The goal of this project is to broadcast a "live" production of the play over the Internet. The play's characters, sets and props are being constructed using VRML 2.0. Some of the characters' avatars can be controlled by motion capture systems. Others will be operated by "puppeteers" working on a variety of workstations. The voices of the characters will be performed live by actors. Because we are interested in the broadcast element of this medium, the audience will be able to watch the play from a variety of viewpoints, including a director's viewpoint that changes position in much the same way that a movie or television production controls the camera angle.

This area is burgeoning with possibilities, as more and more scenic designers move from computer-aided design (CAD) to projecting virtual worlds on stage. Directors and choreographers will find many possibilities inherent in rapid and instantaneous changes of scenery, coupled with the ability to move around virtual spaces in real time. Further information can be found at <http://www.sirius.com/~rat/04.FutureTheater.html>.

MIDI

MIDI is the acronym for Musical Instrument Digital Interface. It is a computer protocol for relaying information about music (notes, duration, tempo, volume) from a computer, to various electronic keyboards and other musical instruments (e.g., drum kits). It can also be used to run lighting systems.

While not a medium for performance itself, MIDI is very useful in theatrical and dance productions. Because the files are small in size (MIDI does not record sound, only binary information), they can be stored and transferred electronically with ease. At the same time, the files are very flexible; they can be played as is, or changed very easily using inexpensive music-editing software. Composers can work at a distance from collaborators, and send the files as E-mail attachments. MIDI files can also be used in rehearsal in place of a rehearsal pianist, and can in fact be used in a production.

While I am not suggesting that MIDI be used to replace live performers, it can be a useful method of creating and sharing music files over the Internet, and can lead to further collaboration of performing artists over long distances. For additional information, contact:

<http://www.leeds.ac.uk/music/Info/MacMIDI/Contents.html>;
<http://home.hwsys.com/users/erics/worldmid/Worldmid.html>.

VIDEOCONFERENCING

So far, I have discussed computer applications that show representations of actors in virtual spaces or that show virtual scenery in real spaces. Video-conferencing software brings the performer (or sometimes several performers) to the screen, but also allows for interactivity. That is, with the proper hardware and software, a video camera and a microphone, audience members can respond to the performers in real time.

Two popular computer applications are used for inexpensive video-conferencing. The first is CU-SeeMe, developed at Cornell University <http://cu-seeme.cornell.edu/>. A color "enhanced" version, developed as a commercial product, is available from White Pine Software <http://www.cuseeme.com/>.

A few years ago, Studio Z <http://www.artswire.org/~studio/> in Chicago created a program called *Voices from Down Under*. Playwrights from both Australia and the United States submitted their plays to begin development with colleagues around the world. Three Australian plays were developed and presented in Chicago, and one American play debuted in Australia. The Chicago presentation was then videotaped and shown on local access TV, and later broadcast (or "netcast") over the Internet using CU-SeeMe video-conferencing software. While this sending of a videotaped program was not interactive, it suggested further possibilities for Internet TV.

Studio Z's latest program, The Playwright in Electronic Residence (PIER), seeks to link playwrights with organizations who wish to produce new plays, but who can not afford to bring a playwright on-site. PIER uses E-mail for communication between director and playwright, but future plans include the use of videoconferencing so that the playwright can be "present" at rehearsals.

J. Matthew Saunders created three performances using videoconferencing while an MFA student at Virginia Tech in Blacksburg, VA. The projects were entitled *The Renaissance Man* <http://dogstar.bevd.blacksburg.va.us/Ren/RenMan1.html>, *The Online Front Porch* and *MobiusTrip*. According to Saunders, the projects were intended to "look at the process of distance collaboration between artists, the possibility of new and diverse audiences, and the opportunity for people to interact in a real, useful and creative way" regardless of distance.

Videoconferencing software has also been used for dance. *soft mirror*, a dance project conceived by Isabelle Jenniches, took place in March of 1998. According to their Web page <http://www.media-gn.nl/mfa/isabelle/Smirror/>, the dancers used live videoconferencing equipment to connect dancer, Beppie Blankert, in the Grand Theatre, Groningen, with Caroline Dokter in de Waag in Amsterdam. The video image was projected onto a big screen to create a (over-/under-) lifesize virtual partner. Fluctuations in transmission and reception rates between the geographically separated participants were embedded in the expression of the performance.

A future project, still in the planning stage is *oudeis, A World Wide Odyssey* <http://www.oudeis.org/>. *oudeis* is "a theatre project that shows Odysseus' journey all around the world on RL [real life] stages and one Cyberstage at the same time, connected via the Internet." Actors on various stages around the world, linked by the Internet and videoconferencing, will present the story of Odysseus, as a performance group literally circles the globe.

CONCLUSION

These initial forays into the uncharted territory of online performance are only the first steps. Though we don't (yet) have the technology to create virtual actors in real space in the way that the *Star Trek* Holodecks do, in the future, cyberspace may well become the site of the performance itself.

WEB SITES

In addition to Web Sites for organizations listed elsewhere in this volume, and those listed previously in this chapter, you may find additional, useful information at the following sites. Use any of the major search engines to look for specific information, and make note of the links you find at the sites you visit. (If you wish to create your own Web Site, contact the Stage Directors and Choreographers Foundation, which creates individual artists' pages and links them to its site <http://www.ssdc.org/foundation>.)

WEB SEARCH ENGINES

Lycos <http://www.lycos.com/>;
Excite <http://www.excite.com/>;
Yahoo <http://www.yahoo.com/>.

THEATRE-RELATED SITES

ARTSEDGE
<http://artsedge.kennedy-center.org/artsedge.html>
ARTSEDGE, The National Arts and Education Information Network, operates under a cooperative agreement between the John F. Kennedy Center for the Performing Arts, the National Endowment for the Arts, and the U.S. Department of Education. Helps artists, teachers and students gain access to information, and share resources and ideas that support the arts.

BuzzNYC
<http://www.buzznyc.com/cgi-bin/homepro.cgi>
Information about theatre in New York City.

Costume World
<http://www.costumeworld.com/>
To buy or rent costumes online.

Directors Agents
<http://www.hollywoodu.com/dagt.htm>
List of agencies that represent directors.

Drama Book Shop
<http://www.dramabookshop.com>
Theatre book store located in New York City. Search this site for books and periodicals.

Drama Resources
<http://wwar.com/theater/dramas.html>
Includes training programs, theatres, cultural foundations, international resources.

Drama Schools and Departments
<http://www.uktw.co.uk/training.html>
UK Theatre—information on performing arts training throughout the UK.

Dramatic Exchange
<http://www.dramex.org/htmlplays.html>
Index of plays.

4Costumes
<http://www.4costumes.com/>
Useful information for locating costumes and accessories.

Howard Jackobs Associates
<http://www.interaccess.com/hja/>
Specializes in public relations, marketing, general management and special events.

Joe Geigel's Favorite Theatre Related Resources
<http://artsnet.heinz.cmu.edu/OnBroadway/links/TheatrePages/edu>
Educational-based theatrical resources.

Los Angeles Times Theatre Page
<http://www.calendarlive.com/LA>
Features theatre news from the *Los Angeles Times*.

Marketing
<http://elaine.teleport.com/~cdeemer/MarketingP.html>
Advice on how to market your play, and get it into the hands of directors, producers, agents, actors.

National Endowment for the Arts
<http://arts.endow.gov/>
Homepage for the National Endowment for the Arts, a federal agency.

National Theater Institute
<http://www.studyabroad.com/nti/letter.html>
Exposes young theatre artists to conservatory-based theatre training, and provides an "orientation" into the professional theatre.

nytheatre.com
<http://www.botz.com/nytheatre/>
Information about the New York City theatre scene (formerly Martin's Guide to New York Theatre).

On Broadway
<http://artsnet.heinz.cmu.edu/OnBroadway/>
Information about current and upcoming Broadway shows. Includes links to shows' individual Web Sites.

Playbill on-Line
<http://www.playbill.com>
Includes news of the theatre industry, databases of biographical information, access to tickets and discounts, plus many other links.

Roundabout Theatre Company
<http://www.roundabouttheatre.org/>
A not-for-profit theatre.

Stage Directions Magazine
<http://www.stage-directions.com/>
Includes hands-on help in every area of community, regional and academic theatre.

Theatre Central
<http://www.playbill.com/cgi-bin/plb/central?cmd=start>
Comprehensive listing of links to theatres and theatre-related organizations around the world.

Theater Magazine
<http://www.yale.edu/drama/publications/theater/>
An informative publication for and about the contemporary stage.

theatre-link.com
<http://www.theatre-link.com/>
A complete index to theatre-related information.

The Tony Awards
<http://www.tonys.org>
The homepage of the annual awards for Broadway theatre, the Antoinette (Tony) Perry Awards; also contains many links.

INDEX

Pirate Playhouse 151
Pittsburgh Public Theater 152
Planco, Johnnie 122
Platform 110
Play Directing: Analysis,
    Communication and Style 45
Play Director's Survival Kit 45
Playbill on-Line 215
Playbill: The National Theatre
    Magazine 63
Playing Director: A Handbook for
    Beginners 46
PlayMakers Repertory Company 152
Playwrights Horizons Theatre
    School 21, 25
Plaza de la Raza 106
POP 163
Portland Center Stage 152
Portland Stage Company 152
Preeo, Max 64
Presenting Opportunities Pilot 163
Primary Stages 153
Primer for Choreographers, A 54
Prince Musical Theatre Program,
    The Harold 31
Printemps des Arts de Monte—
    Carlo 197
Production Notebooks, The:
    Theatre in Process, Volume 1 46
Professional Artists 121
Professional Guest Director/
    Choreographer Program 76, 109
Propp LLP, Tanner 125
Prospector's Choice 70
Pryor, Cashman, Sherman & Flynn 125
Puerto Rican Culture, Institute of 84
Purdy, Marshall B. 177
Quinn Fund, Nancy 91, 163
Quinn, M. L. 47
Raider, Honey 121
Rathacker, Flo 116
Reader's Digest Arts Partners
    Program, Lila Wallace 95
Reed Festival and Workshops for
    the Performing Arts, Donna 23

Regional Artists Project Grants
    Program 76
Regional Organization of Theatres
    South 91
Rehearsal Management for
    Stage Directors 46
Reich, Sacha 34
Repertorio Español: Edward and
    Sally Van Lier Fellowships 76
Résumé Tips 30
Revisionist Stage, The: American
    Directors Reinvent the Classics 47
Rhode Island State Council on
    the Arts 84
Richards, Jeffrey 169
Roberts, Inc., Flora 119
Robinson, Brog, Leinwand, Reich,
    Genovese & Gluck, P.C. 125
Rodger, David 64
Rodgers, Wanda C. 45
Rodner, Esq., Stephen 125
Rogers, James W. 45
Roosevelt University 9
Rose Theater, The 153
Ross, Joe 122
Roundabout Theatre Company 153, 215
Roundtree, Margi 116
Russo, Carole 115
Russo, Jonathan 115
Rutgers: The State University of
    New Jersey 10
Sacramento Theatre Company 153
Sally Van Lier Fellowships,
    Repertorio Español: Edward and 76
Samelson, Judy 63
Samoa Council on Culture, Arts and
    Humanities, American 78
San Diego Performing Arts League 174
San Jose Repertory Theatre 154
Saperstein, Terry 126
Saratoga International Theatre
    Institute 26
Savonlinna Opera Festival 191
SBA 174
Schacter, Elizabeth 116

Sign me up!

For the latest updates to this volume,
don't forget to check the SDC Foundation Web Site frequently:

www.ssdc.org/foundation

For notices of our upcoming events and publications,
sign up for our e-mailing list and/or our regular mailing list
by filling out the form below and sending or faxing it back to us.

Name: _____

Address: _____

City: _____ State: _____ Zip: _____

Phone: _____ Fax: _____

E-mail: _____

We need your feedback!

Help us make the 2nd Edition of the *Stage Directors Handbook* more complete.
Fill out the following form (use additional sheets as required)
and send or fax it back to us.

Corrections:

New Listings:

Other Suggestions:

SDC Foundation
1501 Broadway, Suite 1701, New York, NY 10036;
(212) 302-6195 FAX
Thank you!

The Journal

FOR STAGE DIRECTORS & CHOREOGRAPHERS

"Enriching...Energizing...Enlightening...Essential..."

From nuts-and-bolts guides:

- Who gives money to artists?
- Where do I find good training programs?
- How do I produce my own work?
- How do I find an agent or attorney?
- What are the latest books or periodicals that can help me in my career?

To insights by professionals in the field:

- How do critics look at the work of directors in the field?
- How can directors and choreographers more effectively describe their vision to designers?
- What is the relationship between director and playwright?
- Interviews with such artists as: Anne Bogart, Michael Kidd, David Mamet, Des McAnuff, Harold Prince, Ann Reinking, Susan Stroman, Julie Taymor and Jerry Zaks.

The Journal provides more of what you need. Each issue includes interviews and articles illustrated with photographs, a resource guide, commentary, letters, book reviews and updates on activities for directors and choreographers sponsored by
The Stage Directors and Choreographers Foundation

TCG Individual Membership

You're invited to become an Individual Member of *Theatre Communications Group*— the national organization for the American theatre and the publisher of *American Theatre* magazine.

    As an Individual Member of TCG, you'll get inside information about theatre performances around the country, as well as substantial discounts on tickets to performances and publications about the theatre. Plus, as the primary advocate for not-for-profit professional theatre in America, TCG will ensure that your voice is heard in Washington. We invite you to join us today and receive all of TCG's benefits!

Members Receive These Special Benefits

- A subscription to *American Theatre* magazine—10 issues...5 complete playscripts... artist profiles...in-depth coverage of contemporary, classical and avant-garde performances...3 special issues—including *Season Preview* (October), *Theatre Training* (January) and *Summer Festival Preview* (May).
- Discounts on tickets to performances at more than 230 participating theatres nationwide.
- 15% discount on resource materials including *Theatre Profiles, Theatre Directory, ArtSEARCH* and *Dramatists Sourcebook*—all musts for the theatre professional or the serious theatregoer.
- A catalogue of publications.
- 10% discount on all books from TCG and other select theatre publishers.
- Your personalized Individual Membership card.
- Opportunity to apply for a No-Fee TCG Credit Card.
- Up to 60% off regular hotel rates from Hotel Reservations Network.

TCG Individual Membership

As a Member, You Get a FREE Subscription to <u>American Theatre</u> ...

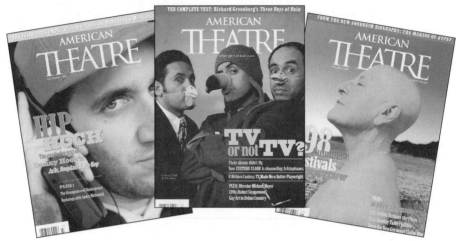

... That's a $49.50 Savings on What You Would Pay at the Newsstand ...

*A*merican Theatre magazine, available 10 times per year, provides up-to-the-minute coverage of the trends, artists and topics shaping American theatre today. In addition to all the articles, you'll also receive five full-length plays—the newest works by prominent playwrights like Tony Kushner, Wendy Wasserstein, Suzan-Lori Parks, David Rabe and Athol Fugard. Plus three special issues including "Season Preview" in October, listing the complete performance schedules for more than 200 theatres across the U.S.; "Summer Festival Preview" in May, listing theatre festivals worldwide; and "Theatre Training" in January, reporting on the opinions, evolution and theory of theatre education in America.

Join Now and Save

Receive 15% Savings Off
TCG Resources ...

- *ArtSEARCH,* TCG's twice-monthly national employment bulletin, with more than 6,000 listings of available jobs for the entire spectrum of the arts each year.
- *Dramatists Sourcebook,* the essential annual guide for playwrights, translators, composers, lyricists and librettists, listing hundreds of fellowships, grants and awards, and submission requirements for more than 350 theatres.

  - *Stage Writers Handbook,* the complete business guide for playwrights, composers, lyricists and librettists, providing the information and ideas necessary to conduct careers in a businesslike manner, along with all the protections the law provides.
  - *Theatre Directory,* a handy pocket-sized annual directory providing contact information for more than 300 not-for-profit professional theatres and dozens of related organizations.

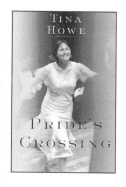

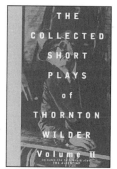

... and 10% Off Other Publications

- Save 10% on all TCG publications as well as theatre books published by Nick Hern, Absolute Classics, Oberon Books Playwrights Canada Press, Aurora Metro Press and Ubu Repertory Theater.

Take Advantage Now and Save!
Become a TCG Individual Member and Receive
Extraordinary Benefits!

☐ **YES**, I would like a one-year Individual Membership to TCG, which includes a subscription to *American Theatre*, among other extraordinary benefits.

    ☐ Individual Membership ~~$35.00~~ $30.00.

    ☐ Student Membership (enclose copy of ID) $20.

☐ I prefer a two-year membership.

    ☐ Individual Membership ~~$70.00~~ $55.00.

**Not only would I like to become a member,
but I would like to take advantage of my discounts right now!**
(Discount prices are only good if you are a member. If you are not a member,
please use the full price for your order.)

    ☐ Please begin my one-year subscription to *ArtSEARCH*.

<u>Individual</u> ☐ with E-mail ~~$64.00~~ $54.40 ☐ without E-mail ~~$54.00~~ $45.90

<u>Institutional</u> ☐ with E-mail ~~$90.00~~ $76.50 ☐ without E-mail ~~$75.00~~ $63.75

☐ **TOTAL ORDER** _____

To order, you may: Send this form to TCG Order Dept., 355 Lexington Ave, NY, NY 10017-0217; or Call (212) 697-5230, ext. 260; or Fax (212) 983-4847; or send E-mail to: orders@tcg.org. Credit card orders: please include your billing address if it is different than your mailnig address.

☐ Check is enclosed. ☐ Please charge my credit card. ☐ VISA ☐ MC ☐ AMEX

NAME		
ADDRESS		
CITY	STATE	ZIP
* PHONE/FAX/E-MAIL		
CARD #		EXP. DATE:
SIGNATURE		
OCCUPATION/TITLE		

   * **all orders must have telephone number**

For Individual Memberships outside the U.S., please add $12 per year (U.S. currency only, drawn from U.S. Bank). Allow 6-8 weeks from receipt of order.   [DSDHBI]